Military Spouse
Finance Guide

Military Spouse Finance Guide

Financial Advice for the Homefront

iUniverse, Inc.
New York Bloomington Shanghai

Military Spouse Finance Guide
Financial Advice for the Homefront

iUniverse books may be ordered through booksellers or by contacting:

iUniverse
1663 Liberty Drive
Bloomington, IN 47403
www.iuniverse.com
1-800-Authors (1-800-288-4677)

Because of the dynamic nature of the Internet, any Web addresses or links contained in this book may have changed since publication and may no longer be valid.

ISBN: 978-0-595-47777-7

Printed in the United States of America

This book is dedicated to the men and women of the Armed Forces, who so bravely serve our country every day, and their families at home who sacrifice so much in the defense of freedom.

Contents

About Pioneer Services
Associates

For more than 20 years, Pioneer Services associates have provided military families with financial education and responsible financial services. By providing service members with the products and knowledge they need, we help the men and women of the Armed Forces focus on their military duties in the field, rather than money problems at home.

With more than 500 combined years of military service, we truly understand what military families go through every day. Our understanding of the military lifestyle contributed to the development of this book, and will continue to be a factor in helping service members take control of their finances.

We dedicate this book to all those who serve, whether on the front lines or the homefront.

Foreword

USA Cares has helped thousands of military families with financial problems. Many found themselves in such situations because of a lack of knowledge when it comes to managing their finances and money, a common dilemma in both the military and civilian sectors.

As a military spouse, it is vital that you have the information necessary to properly manage your family's finances. The Department of Defense and the military services have also recognized this, making financial education and training of service members a top priority.

As you read through the *Military Spouse Finance Guide*, you will find the tools and gain the skills needed to ensure your family's long-term financial success. Better yet, these are tools and skills you can use throughout your life, even after your spouse has left the military. We have learned here at USA Cares that often the solution lies right in front of the family, if only they would have known the information in a timely manner and put it to good use.

I hope you enjoy this informative book and urge you to incorporate its recommendations into your daily routine. Adopting even a few may have a significant impact on your family's financial health.

Thank you for your service and sacrifice for our nation as a military spouse.

Command Sergeant Major Roger Stradley, U.S. Army (Retired)
Founder of USA Cares

Foreword

Military spouses are often the unsung heroes of the military. When the service member is away, the spouse is left in charge of legal and financial issues at home. Family separations are stressful enough; however, when financial concerns are added, that stress is greatly compounded.

One of the best buffers for the challenges of military life is knowledge, and financial knowledge is crucial to all military families. Knowing how to establish and handle credit, whether you're saving enough to be prepared should an emergency strike your family, and how to prepare for future expenses (such as college for the children and retirement) will help your family feel more in control of a life that you may often feel you have very little control over.

This book will provide you with advice that will help arm you with the financial knowledge you need to make smart choices with your money throughout your spouse's military career, as well as after it is over.

Now is the time to learn to take control of your money, rather than having your money control you.

Sylvia Kidd
Director, Family Programs
The Association of the United States Army

Introduction

As a military spouse, you are probably well aware that financial problems can often have an impact on your husband or wife's ability to carry out his or her military duties. Recent reports have highlighted this issue, revealing that financial difficulties could have significant mission impact, such as requiring an individual to return from a deployment to resolve a financial emergency.

If a military family experiences financial difficulty, it can be a long path back to financial stability. This is due to lower than average pay, the near impossibility of service members obtaining a second job, and difficulties with spouses finding employment due to frequent moves.

But research also shows that this problem can be addressed with comprehensive education. By gaining control over your family's finances with some basic knowledge and tips, you can ensure that your Soldier, Sailor, Airman or Marine will be ready when called upon.

This book is intended to act as a reference guide on the fundamentals of personal financial management. Specifically, it focuses on things that you as a military spouse can do to help get your family on a solid financial footing. Stressing both discipline and training, this guide was developed from more than 20 years of experience working with military families and is aimed at helping you better understand your family's finances.

1. **Everyday Spending**—Real-world strategies to find extra money, even in the tightest budget.

2. **The Importance of Your Credit Report**—What a credit report is, how it influences lending decisions, and how military life can affect a credit score.

3. **Reading the Fine Print**—Stresses the importance of comparing checking accounts and fees at different banks and credit unions to find the one that is best for your family.

4. **Smart Borrowing**—Goes through the terms used in lending, and shares strategies to find the true cost of a borrowing decision.

5. **Online Borrowing**—If you borrow money online, there are a few steps to follow to ensure you're getting the best deal.

6. **Bad Borrowing**—Not all lenders are created equal, and this chapter will show you which options to avoid and why.

7. **Debt Prioritization**—Debt is a reality of modern life, but not all debt is the same. Learn which debt is best to pay off early, which can wait, and how to manage it all effectively.

8. **Credit Protection Plans**—What they are, how they should be sold, and what to look for when getting one.

9. **Dealing with Deployment**—How deployment can affect your finances and ways to save money and secure your finances during the process.

10. **Perfecting Your PCS**—Tips on how to financially prepare for a permanent change of station.

11. **Happier Holidays**—Learn how to pay off last year's debt, as well as how to give everyone what they want next year without breaking your budget.

12. **Buying a Car**—You could save thousands on your next car by following a few easy steps.

13. **Simple Tax Tips**—How to prepare for and take advantage of tax planning opportunities for military families.

14. **Preparing for Financial Emergencies**—Why every military family should have an emergency savings account and how to set one up, even with a limited income.

15. **Saving for Retirement**—Takes a look at Thrift Savings Plans and shows why you should start one sooner, rather than later.

16. **Teaching Kids Money Management**—Simple ways to set a solid foundation for a child's future financial success.

17. **College Savings 101**—From education savings accounts to pre-paid tuition, it's never too early to start saving for college.

18. **The Danger of Identity Theft**—How to protect yourself from the nation's fastest growing crime.

19. **Gone Phishing: How to Avoid Online Scams**—We've all received the e-mails assuring us we've won a lottery or have an issue with an account. This chapter shows you how to keep from falling victim to these scams.

20. **Resources**—A list of helpful Web sites and links to sources used in this book.

21. **Glossary**—Definitions of commonly-used financial terms.

The goal of this book is to provide complete, accurate and usable information so every military spouse can gain essential information, be good stewards of their finances, and allow their military husbands or wives to remain focused on their primary mission. The key is to provide the tools and resources so military families can take positive action, because information without execution is meaningless.

Everyday Spending

The formula for financial success is actually quite simple: Earn more than you spend, create positive cash flow, and then save it whenever possible. While this may seem overly simple and at times difficult to do, it can be done if you follow some key steps to manage your day-to-day spending.

Before you can start planning how to pay for college tuition, a house, or retirement, it is important to define your current spending patterns. This will create a baseline that allows you to monitor progress and map a course to financial independence. From there you can set short-term, medium-term and long-term goals. You can then create a budget and, by practicing day-to-day fiscal discipline, achieve your goals.

Attitudes about budgets

Budgets are not only for people who have lots of money or for those whose money doesn't run out each month. Budgets are for everyone, even those who seem to be committed to spending more than they make.

Cutting out a little here and there adds up over time if the discipline learned in the military is applied to money management.

When you think of your budget, look at it as a tool to help you manage, control, and evaluate your spending and saving habits. There will be trade-offs, but budgets aren't just about sacrifice—they are about information, realizing where your money is going and translating that knowledge into the power to change financial behaviors.

Starting a budget

The process of budgeting includes tracking your income and your expenses, and then planning on how to increase your income (if possible) and reduce your expenses.

The basic formula you need to keep in mind is: Income - Expenses = Savings/Debt

- **Income:** The definition of income is any regular payment you receive. Income from your spouse includes base pay, your housing allowance, plus any other special duty or temporary pay. These amounts all show up on your spouse's Leave and Earnings Statement (LES).

- **Expenses:** These are any and all bills you pay, including money set aside in the Thrift Savings Plan, child care, cell phone, Internet, and even food and gifts.

Begin your budget by adding up all sources of income each month. Then, add up your total expenses. The difference will tell you if you need to cut spending and/or increase income, or if you have some extra money to set aside for your medium- and long-term goals. When you are done, the finished product should look something like this:

<u>Income</u>

Monthly net pay after all deductions	$_____
Supplemental pay (BAH, Jump Pay, etc.; Note if temporary)	$_____
Other income (i.e. spouse's income; Note if temporary)	$_____
Interest and/or dividends paid in cash	$_____
Child support	$_____
Alimony	$_____
Other income	$_____
Total Monthly Income...=	$_____

<u>*Expenses*</u>

Emergency savings account	$_____
Thrift Savings Plan	$_____
Mortgage/rent payment	$_____
Utilities (gas, electric, water, and sewage)	$_____
Home-related payments (e.g., maintenance and upkeep)	$_____
Auto loan/lease payment	$_____
Groceries and related home expenses	$_____

Dining out expenses	$_____
Entertainment expense related to fun and family	$_____
Gifts	$_____
Automobile expenses (e.g., gas and tune-up)	$_____
Credit card payments ($ planned to repay monthly)	$_____
Insurance payments (e.g., auto, home, life, and disability)	$_____
Travel or holidays	$_____
Child care	$_____
Telephone	$_____
Clothes and personal items	$_____
Other expenses	$_____
Total Monthly Expenses..=	$_____

Monthly Balance (Income minus expenses)............................= $_____

There are a few hints to consider when formulating a budget:

- **Start slowly**—Begin by focusing on a monthly budget to reach short-term goals. Once you have control, you can become more aggressive in planning medium- and long-term objectives.

- **Be realistic**—Do not over or underestimate your income or expenses. It is better to have a little left over than to have your money come up short at the end of the month.

- **Include all of your regular expenses**—Remember to include bills that you pay annually, biannually, or quarterly. For example, if your car insurance is $1,600 a year, this would amount to $133.33 per month [$1,600 ÷ 12] for your budgeting purposes.

- **Plan ahead**—Have an emergency savings account of around two to three months pay in case of unexpected bills. (Chapter 14: *Preparing for Financial Emergencies*, offers more information on emergency savings accounts.)

Going from debt to savings

After you make your budget, you may find that you do not have the income needed to match your expenses.

Increasing income is a way to solve an unbalanced budget, but active-duty service members may have difficulty getting second jobs, and military spouses sometimes make less than their civilian counterparts due to the military life-style (frequent moves, etc.), so this can be difficult.

The next option is to cut expenses, but you certainly do not want to give up everything you enjoy. If you do, you will not stick to your plan. So how can you make the decisions you must make without giving up everything else in the process?

You can start by following some simple, yet effective, spending strategies to alter your spending patterns.

- **Save on groceries**—Saving on groceries is simple: Plan ahead, make a list, and stick to the list.

  Clipping coupons is another great way to save money. If you save just $5 a week you are saving more than $250 a year. If you don't get the newspaper, you can go online and print out all the coupons you want for free at www.smartsource.com.

  Also, never go food shopping when you are hungry. You may wind up buying items that sound good while you're there, but you may not actually eat when you get home.

- **Build savings with a change jar**—Put your change into a jar each day and periodically visit your financial institution and deposit the money into your savings account. For the more aggressive savers, put one-dollar bills into the same jar to accelerate the saving process.

- **Buy Used**—Did you know that a car loses an average of 20 to 30 percent in value the day you drive it off the lot? A three-year-old car with low mileage can save you 60 percent on the price of the car. For example, a brand new Chevy Malibu is around $26,000, but after three years it could be purchased for less than $12,000. At only two years old, expect the depreciation to be 25 to 75 percent of the original sticker price.

- **Pay cash, or finance smart**—When buying a car, try to pay cash. However, if you do need financing, be sure it is a short-term install-ment loan to minimize interest costs.

  Some may say that financing a new car is less expensive due to lower interest rates. But if that new Malibu ($26,000) is financed at four percent for five years, and the used one ($12,000) is at 14 percent for five years, the monthly cost of the new Malibu is $479 and the used one $279. By buying used you save $200 a month, which is money that you can use to pay off debt or put toward savings.

- **Adjust your insurance**—The average person submits a homeowner's or renter's insurance claim only once every 11 years, and an auto insurance claim every four years. Based on the real risk and the premiums you pay, it is a lot cheaper for you to have a higher deductible and a lower premium.

  It's also a good idea to shop around to make sure you're getting the best rates. Once a year, check out other companies to see if their rates would be lower than what you currently pay.

- **The IRS can be your friend**—The average American family pays 38 percent of its total income for all taxes every year, which is more than they pay for food, shelter, and clothes. So it is important to look for ways to minimize overpaid taxes.

  Re-file past taxes (through an amended return) if you discover you paid too much in previous years. If you owe the IRS, don't send payment until it is due. And if the IRS owes you, file early. The goal is to get your money working for you sooner.

  Also, review your spouse's LES for accuracy—many people select the wrong number of exemptions or dependents. If you get a big refund in April you should consider giving yourself a monthly pay increase by altering your exemptions.

  There are a number of different tax advantages for service members, so visit a tax professional familiar with the military to get more information.

Budgeting savings

Part of any spending plan includes saving money, and the entire concept of saving is to "pay yourself first." This means that you set extra money aside for your future before you make a "want" purchase, such as a new television or the latest fashion trend. Think about the financial implications for every purchase and consider how those same "wants" could be converted into long-term wealth.

If you aren't already there, once you get to the point at which you have a positive monthly balance, put money into a savings plan. Since military pay is often below that of the civilian sector, paying bills first and then finding money to save while avoiding "wants" may seem virtually impossible.

The key is to be disciplined and stick to your budget. Many families benefit from the discipline of a budget, especially writing down their income and taking the time to define all their monthly expenses. Many also soon realize how quickly $5 and $10 purchases add up.

Short-term savings

The first step is to develop an emergency fund for those unexpected expenses that can wreck your budget. Even if you only pay yourself $20 a month, do so before you spend anything on leisure activities or buy something new. Doing so prevents you from having to use a credit card or other financing when you need car repairs, emergency travel home, or have unplanned bills.

Medium-term savings

Next, consider any large purchase coming up in the next five to 10 years. Will you need a new car? New furniture? A down payment for a home? Start putting money aside in an interest bearing, yet easily accessible account to help offset the cost. You may not be able to set aside enough to cover the entire purchase, but you can get closer by putting a few dollars away now.

Long-term savings

Last, look at options for long-term savings—preferably the tax-deductible, tax-deferred Thrift Savings Plan (TSP) offered by the military. What makes this type of plan a good way to save money is the power of compounding interest. When interest earned is added back to the account, rather than paid out to you, the interest itself earns interest. This is the best way to earn money quickly.

While thinking about retirement may seem pointless when you are young, a little money put aside now quickly adds up:

- $1,000 spent on clothes over the course of a year could turn into $17,449 in a 30-year TSP.
- $6 spent each week on double mocha lattes could turn into $56,454 in a 30-year TSP.
- Two fast food meals a week could turn into $91,173 in 30 years in a TSP.
- Your spouse's $7,500 reenlistment bonus could turn into $130,871 in a 30-year TSP.

These numbers not only show the power of compounding interest; they also show that cutting out a little here and there adds up over time if the discipline learned in the military is applied to money management.

Starting a savings program earlier is always better. The following chart shows the power of compound interest when someone puts either $50 or $100 per month into an account or investment that offers a 10 percent rate of return (the average for the stock market over the past 100 years):

Start saving at age	Save this amount/month	Amount saved at age 65	TSP Value at age 65
18		$28,800	$581,395
25	$50	$24,600	$295,426
35		$18,600	$110,213
18		$57,600	$1,162,791
25	$100	$49,200	$590,854
35		$37,200	$220,426

For illustrative purposes only. Figures are based on a 10 percent rate of return.

The key to any long-term strategy is to start early. While rates of return are important, starting early makes the most difference because no matter the rate of return, the longer the money has to earn interest, the more money will be there when it comes time to retire.

Many people neglect to save and wind up with tremendous debt, poor spending habits, and have to work well past retirement age. This is even more troublesome for military families because financial issues can distract a service member from his or her duties. But with a workable plan, the discipline to stick to that plan, and a few changes to your spending and savings habits, you can have financial success for years to come.

The Importance of Your Credit Report

A Soldier was turned down for a car loan request, but wanted to learn more about his credit report. He found several charged off and collection accounts, and there was even one loan that was not his.

His first action was to contact the prior creditors and work toward a payoff or settlement. Then he worked with the credit bureau to remove the debt that was not his. Soon he and his wife both deployed to Iraq, but continued to pay on the old accounts, eventually paying them in full.

Returning from Iraq, the Soldier was surprised to learn that none of those debts or mistakes had been updated on his credit report. So he sent proof to the bureau and submitted dispute letters, eventually getting the items cleared and improving his credit score. All this effort resulted in great news: he was approved for a mortgage, his long-term dream! And all because he got a copy of his report, fixed any errors, and dedicated himself to staying on top of it for the long haul.

Today's global economy and information highway create and retain huge amounts of information about you. Because of this, your credit report is now an essential part of your livelihood. This information is currently warehoused by three major credit bureaus—Trans Union, Experian and Equifax—and their reports create your credit "reputation," so to speak.

Credit score basics

A credit score is a method of determining the likelihood that credit users will pay their bills. Basically, it attempts to condense a borrower's history of paying financial obligations into a single number.

Developing these models involves studying how millions of people have used credit. Through this process the credit bureaus have developed a scoring system that indicates future credit performance.

> *With a typical age of less than 25, multiple addresses in a short period of time and limited income, one can see how a military family might be at a disadvantage—since these all negatively affect a credit score, service members and their families often have artificially low scores.*

How scores are determined

How a credit score was determined (called a "FICO" score after the company that first invented the formula in the 1950s, Fair Isaac Corporation) was a closely held secret by Fair Isaac and the three credit bureaus. But financial experts agreed that, before recent changes, there were certain things that impacted your score:

Factor	Percentage
Payment history	35
Amount owed	30
Length of credit history	15
New credit	10
Type of credit	10

Source: www.myfico.com

The score also considered other factors, such as:

- Late payments.
- The amount of time credit has been established.

- The amount of credit used, versus the amount of credit available.
- Length of time at present residence.
- Employment history.
- Negative credit information such as bankruptcies, charge-offs, collections, etc.

The end result was a single number or score, which typically determined the interest rates an individual could obtain.

A new credit scoring model, called FICO 08, was released in early 2008, and alters the importance given to certain factors. For example, more weight is now given to having different types of credit and less weight is placed on the number of accounts you have.

In addition, the old model had a negative view of "hard inquiries," which occurred when a lender looked at your report when you applied for a line of credit. This was a problem since if you were not approved for the loan—or even turned it down—that hard inquiry could lower your score. FICO 08 is designed to put less emphasis on these hard inquiries, and will also change the impact of other items on your report:

- More emphasis on:
  - o Having a wider variety of credit accounts (positive)
  - o Having high balances on your credit cards (negative)
- Less emphasis on:
  - o Actively using the credit accounts you have (positive)
  - o Applying for new credit accounts (negative)

Another goal of FICO 08 is to alter the way people increase their credit score by "piggybacking." This is when someone with a good credit score adds someone with a poor score on a credit account (usually a credit card) as an "authorized user." Doing so imports the positive payment history of the account into the credit report of the person with a poor credit history and, thus, raises that person's credit score.

This loophole came to light in 2007, when credit repair companies started adding customers' information to the credit accounts of complete strangers with good scores. FICO 08 works around this by ignoring "authorized users" on an account and focusing on the actual account holders, including joint accounts.

Under the old model, military families were often at a disadvantage because they were young, had multiple addresses in a short period of time, and had limited income. All of these factors led to artificially low credit scores. While FICO 08 will help change some of that, military families may still find that their lifestyles lead to scores that may not truly measure their abilities to pay their debts.

Credit scores and risk-based pricing

As noted, credit scores are used as a way to gauge risk, with the lower score being the higher lending risk and the higher score being the lower risk.

The simplest way to understand this prime, non-prime, and sub-prime model is to compare car insurance premiums to interest rates.

Higher Risk Insurance	Higher Risk Loans
First time driver	Inexperienced Borrower
Speeding ticket	Late payments
Minor accident	Charge off loan
DWI	Bankruptcy

At age 16, auto insurance is very expensive (sub-prime) due to the extreme risk. If the driver avoids problems (tickets, accidents, etc.) he can expect to be rewarded with lower insurance costs after age 25 (non-prime). If he further avoids problems, and as he gets older, the costs drop even lower (prime).

The defined risk for the insurer is directly attributed to lack of experience and the probability of a claim for the inexperienced or bad driver. Similarly, the type of interest rate you earn is attributable to your credit history—if you have paid your bills late or not at all, or eventually went bankrupt, then your ability to obtain a lower interest rate (or obtain credit at all) is negatively impacted.

Knowing your credit score

The basic thing to remember about your score is the higher the better. While scores originally went from 350 to 850, all three bureaus announced a program in 2006 called VantageScore. To simplify the process and help consumers better understand their score, the new scores will be grouped based on the familiar academic scale:

- A - 901-990
- B - 801-900
- C - 701-800
- D - 601-700
- F - 501-600

Borrowers with "A" credit will be eligible for the lowest interest rates, while those with an "F" will pay high rates, or might not even be able to get credit at all.

Fair Isaac sued the credit bureaus over VantageScore, claiming the three bureaus had violated anti-trust laws by working together. While no one knows how long the lawsuit will take or what the outcome will be, the thing to remember is that the higher your score, the better, no matter what system is used.

For military families, it is important to note that credit scores are based on the individual—there are no "joint" credit reports. When applying for a loan together, however, both of your credit reports will be reviewed.

Analyzing your credit report

Knowing what is in your credit report is the first step toward building and maintaining good credit. Doing so allows you to avoid some of the problems that can arise.

Incorrect information

The three bureaus do not always contain the same information, so one may have an incorrect account, another may not reflect an accurate payment history, and another may have the wrong address. Each of these can negatively affect your credit score, so it's important to review each of the three reports at least once a year.

Incorrect information can be disputed and the credit bureau is required to investigate the matter within 30 days, remove any incorrect information, and notify any institution that has made a recent inquiry. In some cases you are allowed to have the bureau post a 100-word statement in your report explaining the nature of your dispute.

Correcting this information is vital because your credit information can stay with you for up to ten years. Items from collection agencies, missed payments, and court records (such as bankruptcy, liens and judgments) all stay on your credit history for seven years. In other words, businesses will view the credit choices you make today for years to come, even after your spouse's military career is over. This means good credit decisions and correct information are very important.

Prevent identity theft

The latest threat to your credit comes from theft. Identity theft occurs when someone obtains enough of your personal information to acquire credit in your name. And unless you check your report at least once a year, you may never even know it has happened until you get a call from a bill collector.

You can avoid identity theft by guarding your personal information and routinely auditing your credit bureau for accounts you did not open. If you find any, immediately notify the credit bureau and the creditor to begin an investigation into the fraudulent account.

Another protection is available due to FICO 08: consumers in all 50 states can "freeze" their credit report, something that only a few states used to offer. Freezing prevents anyone from accessing the report, thus preventing criminals from opening new accounts since businesses won't be able to verify credit information.

The downside to freezing a report is that each bureau charges you $10 for the service. You will also need to pay a fee to release the report once the situation is resolved, or if you want to apply for a new credit account.

With more than 41 million credit and identity theft victims and counting, military families are encouraged to verify the accuracy of their credit reports and make sure they only contain their information. Working with certified professionals, military families can repair their credit bureau information and thereby improve their FICO scores. (More information on identity theft is available in Chapter 18: The Danger of Identity Theft.)

How to increase your score

There are a number of factors that can negatively affect credit and lead to an incorrectly low score. Frequent moves or Temporary Duty (TDY) can result in shorter durations at a single location and lead to multiple credit relationships in many cities. Relocation can also lead to poor credit histories, as bills get lost in the shuffle of the move. In addition, many retailers and small loan companies in military communities do not report to a credit bureau, so a very positive history is never reported.

The truth is, no matter what models or scores are used, the military families with the best money management habits will have a better chance of getting credit and at a lower cost. The following are some suggestions that can improve your score:

- **Review your report**—Since just one negative item can affect your score, make sure your report is accurate. You can get a free copy once a year from all three bureaus at www.annualcreditreport.com. Note that this is the only site legally able to give you free copies. There are other sites that claim to, but they have been noted for fraud and charging you a fee.

  Once you get your copy, dispute any accounts that aren't yours, as well as negative items more than seven years old (10 years if you have filed bankruptcy). You may also want to visit a Certified Credit Report Reviewer since these professionals have detailed knowledge on how to read a report.

- **Pay on time**—Even missing a single payment on a single account can lower your score. To prevent this, consider paying bills by allotment, or set up online bill paying through your bank or credit union to have payments sent automatically each month.

- **Keep balances low**—FICO 08 penalizes you for using too much of your available credit, so try to keep it at around 30 percent of the credit limit. For example, if you have a credit card with a $1,000 limit, it's better to keep the balance at $300 than $800. If you find yourself using the card often, but not maxing it out, then call and get the credit limit raised; doing so will lower the percentage of available credit you are using and increase your score.

- **Keep accounts open and active**—In the past, closing unused accounts would lower your score by a small amount. And since some creditors would automatically close accounts that had not been used in some time, some consumers would have their score reduced through no real fault of their own.

  With FICO 08, closed accounts will be a bigger hit to your score because it puts a focus on those who actively use credit (as long as they do so responsibly), as well as on the total amount of credit you are using compared to what is available.

  So keep your older, higher-limit accounts active by charging something each month, then paying the balance in full when the bill arrives.

- **Piggyback the right way**—The new FICO formula, like the old one, does allow you to benefit from someone else's positive credit history, but you must be a "joint account holder." The good thing is that doing so can increase your score almost immediately, as long as the account remains in good standing. The bad things are that you are now jointly responsible for the debt, and you also may have difficulty being removed from the account (an authorized user can be removed with a phone call, whereas a joint account holder will have to fill out a stack of paperwork). So if you do piggyback, make sure the account is in good standing and is one you want to stay on for an extended period of time.

- **Consider an installment loan**—With the old FICO model, you could simply have several credit cards and receive a high credit score. With FICO 08, you get a higher score by having several different types of credit accounts. Because of this, Liz Pulliam Weston, a finance writer for MSN Money, suggests that if you're having issues paying down your credit card debt, an installment loan is "recommended as a way for people with troubled credit to rehabilitate their scores" since it adds variety to your credit choices.

- **Choose the right company**—Avoid borrowing from companies that do not report your history to credit bureaus, and consider using specialty financial services companies that do not have FICO limits or rank restrictions.

Remember that making sure your payment history is reported correctly is your responsibility, so make sure to check it at least once a year. You can obtain a free copy each year by visiting www.annualcreditreport.com. Also, the Federal Trade Commission has excellent information about identity theft at www.consumer.gov/idtheft/.

The key thing to remember about your credit score is that it is used for many different purposes—the price for credit, getting a job, your spouse's security clearances, and even auto insurance can all be based upon a credit score. As long as you keep close tabs, minimize negative information, and take control of your finances, you can have a stellar credit report and the score to go with it.

Reading the Fine Print

While a checking account, debit card, ATM card or credit card are often seen as harmless financial service products, they may be more expensive than you think—do your homework to understand what products are best for your situation.

Military families are encouraged to ask tough questions when obtaining any type of financial service or product, remembering that if it seems to be too good to be true, it probably is. You have to look for things like:

- Minimum balance requirements
- All fees
- Overdraft charges
- Unplanned rate increases
- Rate increases due to late payments with another creditor.

> *Military families are encouraged to ask tough questions when obtaining any type of financial service or product, remembering that if it seems too good to be true, it probably is.*

All of these surprises can be eliminated if you read the fine print and adjust how you will use these financial products.

Checking Accounts

Since military families relocate frequently, it is common for them to have a checking account from their hometowns, or where they enlisted. Selecting the best checking account, however, requires knowing your checking account habits. In order for you to compare accounts at different banks, regulations require banks to supply Truth in Savings Act (TISA) disclosures and fee schedules for accounts at the request of a consumer. Selecting the wrong account or institution can result in unexpected costs.

- **Minimum Fees**—The first question you should ask is whether or not the bank or credit union has rules about minimum balances. It is not uncommon to find a minimum amount to open the account and an average balance requirement to avoid monthly fees. This does not, however, apply to "free" checking accounts, since it is against federal regulations to charge minimum balance fees on such accounts.

- **Bounced Checks/Insufficient Funds**—The next question is the cost of "bouncing" a check and insufficient funds fees. Insufficient funds fees can average more than $25 per returned check. Some banks also charge a fee for each day an account is in a negative balance position.

- **Overdraft Protection**—You also have to ask questions for accounts with overdraft protection, including everything to which that protection applies. A recent example involved a service member who went to his ATM and requested $20. Despite the fact that he only had $10 in the account, the ATM gave him the money. The account was then charged $17.50 for that overdraft protection. In effect, this was $17.50 in interest to "borrow" $10 that he still had to repay. So make sure that you know the cost of such a transaction and how your bank makes overdraft protection funds available.

- **ATM Fees**—Some institutions charge fees at their ATM's, and when you withdraw from an ATM not owned by them, you can expect a "foreign ATM fee." These surcharges range from $1.50 to $4 per transaction, so be sure to know the fees involved with your ATM card or any ATM machine you use.

The TISA disclosure and fee schedule for each checking account are required to provide the above information and more, and to allow comparison from bank to bank and account to account. By collecting and reviewing these disclosures, you can choose the account that is best for your situation.

Credit Cards

Credit card solicitations appear in your mailbox and the offers look tempting. But then you find that you are charged unexpected fees, or discover that your interest rate isn't what you anticipated.

First is the legal reality. When you signed up for the credit card you were warned in advance. While the font may have been small or the details hidden in pages of disclosures, they did technically inform you that they could raise interest rates, shorten grace periods or unilaterally change the relationship for their benefit.

Second, you can avoid all those solicitations by calling 1-888-5OPT-OUT, or going online to www.optoutprescreen.com. While this won't completely stop all credit card offers, it can significantly reduce the number you receive.

> **You can stop credit card offers by calling 1-888-5OPT-OUT, or going online to www.optoutprescreen.com.**

Here are some of the details you might want to investigate before getting a credit card:

- **Variable rate or APR**—The initial rate offered may increase after an introductory period or when they increase their "base rate."

- **Grace periods**—The original disclosure, or periodic updated disclosure, defines the number of days before interest is charged on a new purchase. If the grace period for making payments is 28 days on the initial offer, then you know when to pay your bill to avoid extra interest and fees.

- **Late payments**—Beyond basic fees like $25 for late or returned payments, a credit card company can automatically raise your interest rate if you miss two payments or are late twice. This can even happen on another card you own, but were not late in paying—this is called "universal default," where a late payment on one account can raise the interest rate from another company.

- **Over credit limit**—You are charged this fee if your balance exceeds the approved credit limit. For example, if you had a $2,000 credit limit and, during a permanent change of station, charged enough to make the total $2,020, you could expect a fee. This fee could be $10 to $20 in addition to the other costs related to the card and purchases.

Checking accounts are useful, and in the world of the Internet, both credit cards and debit cards are almost necessary. Selecting the right account and the right organization, however, is vital to paying only what you should. And to do that, you have to read the fine print and avoid all excess fees.

Smart Borrowing

A Sergeant brought four separate revolving credit cards to the table with true interest rates ranging from more than 19 percent to 27 percent. He was making minimum monthly payments on all four debts. When he learned how to calculate the long-term cost of staying the current course, the service member realized that his current balances of $5,186 would end up costing over $46,289 to fully repay, and would have taken more than 30 years to do so.

With that powerful and eye-opening educational experience, he was ready to take action. By paying off those revolving credit cards with a single and responsible installment loan at a lower rate, the Sergeant could repay the debts in just 30 months. The total payback of $8,080, including all interest and disclosed fees, saved him more than $38,208.

More often than not, when expenses exceed your income, debt is created. But before taking on any type of debt, make sure it is necessary and, if so, only get what you actually need.

One rule of thumb is that debt should not exceed 20 percent of you and your spouse's take-home pay. Another way to handle debt is to set a threshold—for example, no more than 40 percent total debt ratio (all debts divided by take-home pay). The key is to know how much debt is reasonable and set a plan to give yourself a better chance of repaying it—without debt management or proper debt planning, a family can soon find themselves in a debt cycle that can cause damage for years to come.

Avoid the debt cycle

To determine if your family is in the debt cycle, ask yourself a few questions:

- Am I depleting my savings?
- Am I making minimum payments on my credit cards?
- Am I being charged overdraft fees on my bank account?
- Am I being charged late payment fees on any loan?

If you answer "Yes" to any of these questions, there is a good chance your family is currently in the debt cycle. In order to get out of it, there are several key things you should know about borrowing money.

The true cost of borrowing

Using credit to pay for purchases is a fact of life in today's economy. Before you're caught in a financial crisis, however, it's worthwhile for you to learn how to accurately evaluate various lending options. Why? Because all loan options are not the same. In the haste of the moment, when you're desperate for cash, you may not be paying enough attention to what a loan is really costing you.

Rate comparison

One way to compare different types of borrowing is to compare interest rates or annual percentage rates (APR). The problem with doing so is that the term, or length, of the loan is just as important in figuring out the actual cost.

For example, a 90-day $300 loan at 34.95 percent is often seen as a bad decision, while borrowing $300 at a cost of $17.34 is a much better deal. The problem is that these numbers represent the exact same loan and the exact same cost.

So what happens when you need that $300 right away and there are no friends or family members to lend you the money? Do you use a credit card cash advance? A signature loan from a bank, credit union or finance company? How do you know which option is best?

The answers are not so simple, because there are many factors that play a part in the decision: availability, likelihood of approval, convenience, confidentiality, disclosure of proposed loan terms, and of course, whether the loan is fairly priced. For example, borrowing $300 for two weeks at a cost of $20 may be a good deal if done once, but a horrible decision if renewed every other week for several months.

Term comparison

The term, or length, of a loan is another way to compare borrowing choices. For example, if you had two loans of $5,000, at an interest rate of 10 percent, but one was for three years and another for six, the six-year loan would cost you less a month, but wind up costing almost twice as much in total interest paid ($808 for the three-year loan, compared to $1,669 for the six-year loan).

The key here is that you cannot just focus on rates and fees alone when determining the real cost to you, especially when borrowing over a short period. The term of the loan must also be considered when comparing costs.

Know the disclosures

There are several laws designed to help you better understand the fees and other costs associated with obtaining credit.

- **The Truth in Lending Act (TILA) and Regulation Z**—Passed by Congress in 1968, TILA provides a uniform manner of calculating and presenting the terms of consumer loans. It mandates specific disclosures that enable you to compare costs in order to help you make informed credit choices.

- **The Consumer Credit Act of 1974**—This law developed APR calculations in order to provide a standardized formula for determining loan costs. Today, APR disclosures must comply with the Truth in Lending Act and Regulation Z, which means the total cost of a loan must reflect interest charges, loan fees and points.

- **The Fair Credit and Charge Card Disclosure Act**—This was passed in 1988 to further ensure uniform disclosure of rates and costs.

The last law requires all issuers of credit (including banks, credit card companies, and loan companies) to provide consumers with disclosures that must be provided with applications and pre-approved solicitations:

- The APR charged for purchases made on credit, cash advances or balance transfers.

- How the APR is determined and whether or not it is variable.

- The method the issuer uses to compute the balance for purchases where a finance charge is imposed (calculating an average daily balance or using the outstanding balance at the beginning of the billing cycle are examples of such methods).

- The amount of any type of annual fee.
- The amount of any minimum or fixed finance charge that could be imposed.
- Any transaction fee, whether a specific dollar amount or percentage, for purchases.
- Transaction fees for cash advances, and fees for paying late or exceeding the credit limit.
- The amount of any fee imposed to transfer an outstanding balance.
- Whether there is a grace period, and if so, its length.

While these disclosures are helpful, they still may not reflect the true cost of credit. Consider a $100 loan for 14 days, with a $25 fee. The disclosed annual percentage rate is 651 percent. This may seem like an excessively high interest rate, but the reality is simply the $25 cost. A bank might charge you the same $25 if you "bounced" a check. This bank fee does not require a TILA disclosure, but if you calculated the APR, it would exceed 3,000 percent.

Make sure you read all the disclosures and know what fees you may be charged in the future so you are not hit with any surprise costs.

The truth about credit cards

Comparing the true cost of a credit card can be conflicting and confusing, and much has been written to better educate consumers about the true nature of credit card debt.

Beyond interest rates, fees, grace periods, and balance calculations, a recent concern has been minimum payment amounts and the length of time for full repayment. Elected leaders, non-profit organizations and businesses have recently begun education efforts to help consumers better understand costs associated with long-term credit card debt.

To highlight some truth about credit cards, take three examples:

- If you had $1,000 of credit card debt at 17 percent interest, and only made the minimum payment of four percent of the balance, it would take you 84 payments—seven years—to pay off. During that time, you will have paid nearly $500 in interest.
- If you had $2,500 of credit card debt at 17 percent interest, and only made the minimum payment, it would take you 119 months (nearly 10 years) and cost you almost $1,300 in interest.

- If you owed $5,000 at 17 percent interest, and only made the minimum payment, it would take you 145 months (12 years) to pay in full and cost you an additional $2,665 dollars in interest.

You can find out how long it will take you to pay off your credit card debt by using the online calculators at www.pioneermilitarylending.com, as well as at www.cardweb.com and www.bankrate.com.

Another way to look at credit cards is to analyze where your payment actually goes. If you had $5,000 of credit card debt, were late on your payments, and just made the minimum payment ($100 per month), your money wouldn't actually be going to pay off your purchases:

Category Applied To	$100 Payment	What's Left
Late charges	$15	$85
Unpaid finance charge	$28	$57
Fees; (ex: over limit fee, returned checks etc.)	$10	$47
Outstanding balances previously billed (ex: $1,000)	$47	$0.0
Current cash advances and purchases.	$0.0	N/A

In this example, a $100 payment didn't even touch the cash advance and purchase balance. Late fees, over the limit fees and other finance charges ate into the payment so much there was little to nothing left. This is the reason a consumer who only makes minimum payments can spend years paying off credit cards.

The truth about payday lending

According to the Center for Responsible Lending (CRL), nearly all payday loans are made to borrowers with five or more payday loans per year, while hardly any are made to one-time emergency borrowers. The CRL also noted that, prior to restrictions on payday lending to the military, one in five military families had used a payday loan service, with the average payback amount for a $300 loan at $800, and the APR averaging around 400 percent.

When one looks at the true costs, payday loans are simply not a financially sound way to borrow money.

THE TRUE COST OF BORROWING: PAYDAY LOAN vs. INSTALLMENT LOAN		
TYPE OF DEBT	PAYDAY LOAN	INSTALLMENT LOAN
Initial Amount	$500	
APR	730%	24%
Monthly Payment	$650 due in two weeks	$89.26 per month
Total Interest/ Fees Paid	$150	$35.56
Total Amount Paid	$650	$535.56
Time to Pay Off	Two (2) weeks but is "rolled over" into another loan if not paid off in two weeks.	Six (6) months with no rollover allowed

This chart is for illustrative purposes only. The actual payments, interest rates, and dollar amounts you may owe on similar debt may be different than the numbers listed here. The laws regarding payday lending vary from state to state, so the amount you owe may vary depending on where you live.

Source: Pioneer Services

One of the main issues with this type of lending is "rolling over" or "flipping" because of an inability to repay. This can start you and your family on a financially dangerous cycle of debt.

Most cash-strapped borrowers who get payday loans are not able to repay the whole loan within two weeks, and end up rolling over their loan and paying renewal fees multiple times. Trapped on this "debt treadmill," military families typically paid much more in fees than the amount they originally borrowed. This is the reason Congress passed the Military Lending Act, which barred lenders from charging service members and their dependents more than 36 percent APR on any payday, car title, or refund anticipation loan. This has essentially made payday lenders "off limits" for military families.

The key question that every military family in a financial emergency should ask: "If I don't have the $500 today, what are the chances I'll have the money in two weeks?" If the answer is "slim to none," the rollover cycle is bound to begin.

Protect yourself from predatory practices

In the past few years, the subject of predatory lending has become more visible than ever and usually refers to easy-to-get loans that are intentionally structured to be deceptive and hurtful to borrowers.

One thing to note is that predatory lending is a "practice," not a characterization of a particular type of financial institution or where the institution is located. A common belief is that predatory lending to military personnel is an "outside the gate" issue created by small or unscrupulous lend-

One thing to note is that predatory lending is a practice, not a characterization of a particular type of financial institution or where the institution is located.

ers. That belief is, in fact, false. These practices can also occur in businesses that operate on military installations. Location is irrelevant.

Predatory lending can be defined as excessively high annual percentage and interest rates (usually in the triple digits), practices that generate excessive fees, or deliberate deception to conceal the true costs of the transaction. Predatory lending can be found in numerous financial sectors, including credit cards, mortgages, and consumer finance.

Customers who fall victim to such predatory practices quickly find themselves in a seemingly endless cycle of debt. Consider the APR comparisons in the following chart:

Transaction	Annual Percentage Rate*
$100 payday advance with $15 fee	391%
$26 late fee on a $100 credit card balance	678%
$48 Non-sufficient Fund/Merchant fee on a $100 bounced check	1,251%
$50 late/reconnect fees on a $100 utility bill	1,304%

Calculated on a 2-week term

Using this data, it is easy to see that predatory lending is not associated with a particular institution or where that institution is located. If you pay your utility bill late, the fees are astronomical when calculated as an APR over a two-week period and many may consider that predatory.

Some banks do the same thing with "bounce protection" or "overdraft privilege" on checking accounts. Consumer groups such as CRL consider these fees "predatory" because they are, in essence, a "loan" to cover the cost of the check. Some of the other issues CRL has with these fees include:

- **How they occur**—CRL conducted a study and claimed that a few banks "manipulate the order in which they clear deposits and withdrawals in order to maximize overdrafts." In other words, some banks will hold deposits until *after* they've cleared checks, rather than processing transactions by date and time, in order to cause more overdrafts.

- **No notice of insufficient funds**—If someone wishes to withdraw money from an ATM, many banks will allow the transaction to occur regardless of the amount actually in the account at the time. CRL is working to make it mandatory for banks to notify customers when an ATM withdrawal will put an account "into the red."

- **Consumer permission**—Some banks will enroll a customer in an overdraft protection plan without that customer's consent.

Banks counter these criticisms by noting that these fees occur only once, while other forms of lending (such as payday loans) are revolving debts that can cost more. They also point out that the fees keep the check from going back to the retailer, which could lead to more fees and even criminal prosecution.

What to ask when borrowing money

When you have to borrow money, you should ask all of the right questions, insist on full disclosure, and know the true costs and terms to ensure that you are making an informed decision. Without complete information, what looks like a good deal may in fact be a bad one.

- Are you getting full disclosure? A quality lender will tell you upfront about the interest rate and APR, as well as any fees associated with your loan. A predatory lender most often will not.

- Does the company calculate your debt ratio? If they don't, they are not checking to see if you can truly repay the loan.

- Does the company review your credit report with you? This will ensure its accuracy and identify all past and current debt obligations.

- Does the company report your payments? Your best chance to improve your credit score is to prove you can pay your obligation on time and in full. If the company doesn't report positive payment information to a credit bureau, it could be predatory.
- Does the company offer financial education? Make sure the company you are working with has a goal of having better-educated, long-term customers who can successfully manage their finances.
- Does the company always say "yes" to every loan request? Make sure the company you are working with does not approve all applications.

These questions can help ensure that you are fully informed and are making the best choice for you and your family.

Online Borrowing

When it comes to borrowing money online, you should be educated and ready to ask key questions regarding any transaction. There are twelve quick and easy steps you can take to ensure that your transaction goes smoothly and that the money you need today doesn't come back to haunt you tomorrow.

1. Is it a "real" company, or just a Web site?

Legitimate companies and sites will have an actual physical address. This "real life" contact information (a physical address and/or telephone number) should be easily found on their site. But don't just take their word for it—call the number or check online yellow pages to ensure that it's not fake.

Using the Internet to borrow money is a very convenient option that has many benefits. It is important, however, to do some simple homework to ensure that you are dealing with a reputable company.

2. Location, location, location

As a military spouse, you are protected by several laws and regulations at both the state and federal level, but they only apply to companies within the United States. So even if the company has a real address, make sure the company is incorporated within the United States. Doing so allows you to take advantage of these appropriate lending laws and legal protections.

3. Does the lender conform to the Truth in Lending Act?

Always make sure that the lender tells you what your interest rate and Annual Percentage Rate (APR) will be before finalizing the agreement. Since all rates should be based on your credit history, the rate should not automatically be the same for every borrower. If the lender does not tell you the rate—or does not disclose it clearly—it is always best to walk away and find a more upfront and honest lender.

4. Protect your privacy

The company's privacy policy should be offered on their site, and easily accessible, even before you start the application process. Of course, such information is only useful if you actually read it, so take the few minutes and find out how the company will use, share, and protect that information before entering into any agreement.

5. Does the company offer paying by allotment?

Paying by allotment is easier, faster, and prevents you from losing or forgetting a bill during a move. It is, however, illegal for a lender to make it a requirement and should never factor into a loan decision. Just remember that if given the option, it can be a great benefit.

6. Make sure the site is safe and secure

There are two ways to tell if the site you are using is secure once you begin the application process: 1) There should be a yellow "padlock" icon at the bottom of your browser window that indicates you are on a secure connection; 2) the Web address should start with "https" instead of just "http." Also, depending on the browser you are using, you should get a "warning" window informing you that you are using a secure Web page.

7. Check for the Better Business Bureau (BBB) online program

If the Web site has a "BBB Reliability Program" logo on its site, click the logo and see if it takes you back to the BBB site, since the logo can easily be copied and pasted into any random site. While you're there, spend a few minutes and search using the company's name to see if any complaints have been filed and how (or if) they were resolved.

8. Does the lender make sure you can repay the debt?

Any company you borrow money from should be worried about giving you more debt then you can handle. If they don't factor your debt ratio (how much you owe vs. how much you earn), then they probably are not worried about your ability to repay the debt. It is up to you to pay the loan back, so make sure you are dealing with a lender that won't get you in over your head.

Any company you borrow money from should be worried about giving you more debt then you can handle. If they don't factor your debt ratio...then they probably are not worried about your ability to repay the debt.

9. Look for a satisfaction guarantee

Any company confident in its product will offer some type of no-questions-asked satisfaction guarantee. Lending should be no different, especially when you consider the impact a bad borrowing decision can have on your finances.

10. Does the site make financial education information readily available?

Legitimate lenders want consumers to make smart long-term financial decisions. By making financial information and educational materials readily available on their site, these lenders recognize the importance of protecting not only potential customers, but themselves as well. Since you may often find yourself in charge of your household's finances due to deployments, you should take advantage of such education programs.

11. Protect your credit report

Whatever online lender you use should report your positive payment history to at least one of the major credit reporting companies (Experian, TransUnion and Equifax). This is important because some lenders will only report negative items. If possible, ask the company what their reporting policies are by phone, or even by live chat if offered. Beware of companies who do not do any credit reporting at all.

While these tips are in no way all-inclusive, they are easy to follow and can help secure your transaction. Using the Internet to borrow money is a very convenient option that has many benefits. It is important, however, to do some simple homework to ensure that you are dealing with a reputable company. Doing so can not only get you the money you need, but also start a long and beneficial relationship between you and your lender.

12. The rise of peer-to-peer lending

There has recently been a growth in what is called "peer-to-peer" borrowing, where one person loans money at an agreed upon rate to another person, usually online. Each site works a bit differently, but all allow you to set your own interest rate and rely on its members to either accept or decline your request.

Your payments are usually sent through the site, not directly to an individual, and each has a different method of dealing with delinquent borrowers, with most reporting your payment history to the credit bureaus. There is also no formal "approval" process, as found with typical lenders, that sets the rate, so you have to put thought into your request. If you ask for too low a rate, no one will lend you money, while too high a rate could wreck your budget.

The best advice for this type of borrowing is to thoroughly research all of the different sites, find out how their processes work, and look into complaints that have been lodged (if any). Remember that you're doing business with a group of individuals who are choosing to loan you money, instead of a company, so it's a different process than you have probably experienced. It also may take longer than a traditional lender (usually a few weeks, rather than a few days) so keep that in mind.

Bad Borrowing

Almost everyone has found themselves short of cash at some time or another—car repairs, a higher-than-expected utility bill, or overzealous holiday spending can all throw a budget out of line and cause financial panic.

Situations like these are why it's important to have an emergency savings account (see Chapter 14: Preparing for Financial Emergencies, for more information on emergency savings accounts). But if you don't, it's important to make a smart financial decision and choose a responsible alternative. This can mean going to a military relief agency to see if they can provide you with low-cost assistance, visiting your bank or credit union to see if they have options for you, or using a loan company that conforms to all federal lending requirements.

One thing you do not want to do is choose an option that could easily land you in a far worse financial situation.

The definition of predatory lending

While there is no legal definition of "predatory" lending, several non-profit groups like the Center for Responsible Lending, as well as the Federal Deposit Insurance Corporation (FDIC) and the Department of Defense (DoD) have come up with a few general guidelines for what makes up a predatory loan.

The following are all regarded as predatory when distinguishing the difference between responsible lending (including subprime loans) and predatory lending.

- **Failing to ensure a borrower can repay the loan**—All three questionable borrowing options listed below (payday, car title, and refund anticipation loan [RAL]) are not based upon a credit score, debt ratio, or any other factor that shows a customer's ability to repay the debt.

    Often, all that is needed to get these loans is a bank account and a pay stub or, in the case of car title lending, the title to your car.

- **Allowing and/or encouraging rolling over a loan**—According to a study by the Center for Responsible Lending (CRL), 90 percent of payday lending business is to borrowers who flip their loans five or more times. Statistics for car title loans are similar.

  The difference between a "rollover" and a "refinance" it is that a rollover only benefits the lender due to the added fees. A refinance helps the borrower by lowering a rate or monthly payment, or by paying off other debt in the process.

- **Concealing the true cost of the loan**—All three types of lenders that follow often do not share or try to conceal the fact that, when factored as an Annual Percentage Rate (APR), their loans are as high as 700 percent.

  Their argument is that since their loans are only for a short time (from two weeks to one month), they should not have to state the APR. But APR is one of the best ways consumers can gauge the cost of credit, and hiding or making it difficult to find APR information is a disservice to consumers.

As you can see, payday lenders, car-title lenders and RALs all fit most, if not all, of the definitions of predatory as outlined by the FDIC and DoD.

On the other hand, most subprime lenders (those who serve customers with incomplete or less-than-stellar credit histories) check credit reports, do not allow rollovers, and conform to the Truth in Lending Act (TILA) and other federal disclosure guidelines, so customers know the true cost. This is an important distinction when looking for short-term funds since you may need to go to a subprime lender. The key is to ensure you are not going to a *predatory* lender.

Payday Lending

What it is

A payday loan is a short-term (usually two weeks) loan of several hundred dollars. The customer usually writes a check for the amount, plus any fees, and the lender holds the check until the borrower's next payday.

When that next payday comes, the customer can either let the lender cash the check, or the borrower can roll the loan over—which leads to more fees—or, depending on state or local laws, take out an entirely new short-term loan.

Why it's so dangerous

Perhaps the most dangerous part of payday lending is the practice of repeatedly rolling over the loan. This happens when a borrower cannot pay back the initial loan in the designated two weeks, leading to another loan with the same company with even more fees.

A 2003 study by CRL found that just one percent of all payday loan borrowers took out just one payday loan. The remainder took out an average of more than five loans just to pay back the first one, leading to more than $4.2 billion in excessive fees. And this doesn't include those customers who take out a payday loan from another payday loan company—or even several—to pay back another.

One of the reasons for this is suggested by CRL:

> *The prospect of bouncing the check left in the hands of the lender, often accompanied by fear of criminal prosecution for writing a "bad check," puts tremendous pressure on the borrower to avoid default. So the borrower generally pays another fee, typically $50 on a $300 loan, to renew or float the loan for another pay period.*

Combine that with the embarrassment some feel at having financial difficulties, and getting out from under the weight of such a crushing cycle of debt can be incredibly difficult.

Another thing that makes rollovers so dangerous is that the original amount borrowed is never actually paid down. Instead, by continually adding fee upon fee upon fee, the amount continues to go up without the balance ever going down—the debt just keeps climbing, as do your payments. There have been numerous horror stories in the news of people who went in to borrow a few hundred dollars and wound up owing thousands of dollars months later.

Again, this practice makes payday lending incredibly dangerous for your family's finances and can risk your spouse's operational readiness.

Location is not everything

In states where payday lending is legal, payday loan stores outnumber McDonald's, Starbucks and Wal-Marts … *combined.* And a study done in 2005 by the University of Florida showed that payday lenders cluster outside of military bases in higher numbers than in civilian areas.

This does not mean that lenders "outside the gate" are bad—there are many reputable lending institutions not located on military installations. It does mean, though, that ease of access does not mean ease of repayment. So when looking for a short-term loan, do not simply drive to the first place you see.

Yes, you may be in a time crunch and need money soon. But almost every single creditor—whether a repair shop, utility company, or even credit card company—will understand if you call them and explain your situation. If you tell them you are making sure you are getting the best deal in order to pay your debt without ruining your financial future, odds are they will understand and may even give you some assistance.

So find out about the company first, find out what the terms and rates are, and make sure you are getting the best rate given your credit history and budget. If possible, see if the company has some sort of guarantee or return policy so if you do find a better loan, you can take the money back within a certain amount of time.

Off-limit lenders

In recent years, many military leaders declared payday lenders off-limits. This is because financial issues were one of the biggest reasons service members lost their security clearances. The DoD still considers predatory lending one of the top 10 issues hampering operational readiness, and wants those serving in the field to think about their duties, not money problems at home.

Federal lawmakers responded to these concerns by passing the Military Lending Act, which took effect October 2007. This provision puts in place a 36 percent APR cap on payday, car title, and refund anticipation loans given to service members, their spouses and dependents. While this may seem to have made these types of loans a thing of the past for military families, they can still alter their product to get around the law, or operate on the Internet through companies outside of the United States so that they are not bound by federal lending rules.

In order to steer clear of trouble with your finances, as well as your spouse's commanding officer, it's probably best to avoid payday lenders all together.

Car title lending

What it is

A car-title loan is a short-term loan (usually for 30 days) of several hundred dollars where the customer uses his or her car to secure the loan. The loans are usually for less than the car is worth, and if a customer cannot pay back the loan, then the loan can be rolled over (again, with more fees) or the lender will take possession of the car and sell it for a profit.

Car title lending is illegal in most states, but has grown significantly in states where it is still legal. Also, many states have certain laws regulating secured loans, so car title loans are often labeled as "sales and leasebacks" or "pawns" so that lenders can charge triple-digit interest rates.

Why it's so dangerous

Reliable transportation is absolutely vital for military families, so putting your vehicle at risk for a short-term financial emergency is simply not a wise decision. Just how much of a risk is it?

More than 17,000 cars were repossessed due to such loans in 2004, just in the state of Tennessee. Nationally, hundreds of thousands of customers have lost their cars after taking out a car title loan and not repaying it in time.

The CRL points out what makes these loans so dangerous:

> Because the loans are structured to be repaid as a single balloon payment after a very short term, borrowers frequently cannot pay the full amount due on the maturity date and instead find themselves extending or "rolling over" the loan repeatedly. In this way, many borrowers pay fees well in excess of the amount they originally borrowed. If the borrower fails to keep up with these recurring payments, the lender may summarily repossess the car, often stripping borrowers of their most valuable possession and only means of transportation.

In short: Your family's car is too valuable to be put at risk, so don't.

Tax refund anticipation loans

What they are

Refund anticipation loans (RALs) are short-term cash advances against a customer's anticipated income tax refund. Offered through companies that provide tax preparation services and some lenders, they are heavily marketed as a way to get a refund faster.

Why they are so dangerous

There are several issues with RALs that make them something your family should avoid:

- **Fees**—According to a report from the National Consumer Law Center, the effective APR when all the fees are added in can be more than 700 percent. And since the fees are flat and not dependent upon the size of your refund, you pay the same, whether you are getting $100 or $10,000.

- **It's not that fast**—If you file online and have the IRS direct deposit your refund, a RAL will only get the money to you five days earlier. If you're in a money crunch, simply call your creditors and let them know your situation. Chances are they will understand.

- **You're borrowing your money**—By getting a RAL, you are paying someone else a fee to get your money. It's like your spouse paying the Department of Defense a fee each week just so he can get access to his paycheck on the twelfth of every month instead of the fifteenth.

- **"Anticipation" is the key word**—These types of loans are based on what the lender thinks you will receive in a refund, not what you will actually get. There is a chance you could get a RAL that is more than your refund, meaning you will owe the lender more than you get back from the IRS, putting you deeper in a financial hole.

These types of loans, much like payday and car title loans, have come under increasing scrutiny in recent years, with one large company being sued because of the fees and sales practices used with them.

The key thing to remember with RALs is that this is already your money—why pay someone else a fee just to get it a few days sooner?

Better alternatives

Instead of going to a payday lender, getting a car title loan, or an advance on your tax refund, the following are short-term and relatively quick options that can get you the money you need without putting your family's finances in jeopardy.

- **Military relief agencies**—Every branch has them, and they all have some sort of no- or low-interest loan for families with financial emergencies. They should be the first place you go.

- **Non-profits**—Organizations such as USA Cares (www.usacares.us) offer small-dollar grants to families in dire need. They also offer quick turnaround for those who need immediate help. Check your local area to see if there are local agencies that can help.

- **Bank or credit union**—In 2007, the FDIC requested that banks and credit unions offer more responsible alternatives to payday loans. While some have offered these for a while, the federal government is starting a push for such options on a national level, which should provide you with many more choices.

- **Military loan company**—Many military loan companies offer some sort of short-term loan option with rates comparable to a credit card, but with a shorter term (meaning that, unlike a credit card, you'll pay less overall interest).

- **Call the creditor**—If all else fails, call whomever you owe money to and explain your situation. By being proactive, as well as being a military spouse, you may be surprised how willing they are to work with you in figuring out a payment plan. Sometimes, there may not even be a penalty or interest charge.

Any way you add it up, payday, car title, and RAL lenders simply are not responsible financial choices for you and your family. They simply cost too much, can too easily trap your family into a cycle of debt, and can put your spouse's military career at risk.

Debt Prioritization

Credit is a fact of American life. Whether it's a credit card, mortgage, car payment, or even a business needing extra funds to make a new product, almost all of us look to various forms of borrowing to get what we need and want.

The thing to remember is that not all credit is bad. It's how that credit is treated, prioritized, and paid off that makes the difference.

It can be difficult for the average consumer to organize debt effectively—confusion about interest rates versus Annual Percentage Rates (APR), not knowing payoff amounts for certain debts, and the need to balance monthly payments with long-term financial goals can make the entire process too time consuming and hard to grasp.

There are some strategies, however, that anyone can use to prioritize debt and start conquering that mountain of bills. Which ones you use will depend on your own financial status, your goals, and other such factors. But regardless of the strategies you employ, the key is to start now and start making sense of your debt.

Also note that in this chapter, "debt" includes more than just loans or credit cards—it's any revolving, recurring bill you have each month. For this reason, utilities and even rent are classified as "debt."

Paying off debt

If you're not having issues making your monthly payments and just want to reduce your debt load—or you see a day coming when paying bills will be difficult, such as when extra pay ends (combat pay, for example)—there are several different ways to do so.

Which one you choose will depend on your current financial situation, and mixing and matching methods from each is also effective.

Long-term strategy

This strategy looks at which bills will cost the most over time. The goal is to pay the least amount overall, over the course of years, rather than worrying about month-to-month costs. It's the most fiscally responsible way to pay off debt, since it reduces the amount of interest you pay overall.

With this strategy, you look at the total amount paid throughout the lifetime of the obligation, including interest and annual fees. For this reason, credit cards should be at the top of the list when using this strategy.

Using the examples from "Chapter 4: Smart Borrowing" to once again show how much credit cards cost over the long haul, you can see why they should be your primary focus when using this strategy:

- If you had $1,000 of credit card debt at 17 percent interest, and only made the minimum payment of four percent of the balance, it would take you 84 payments—seven years—to pay off. During that time, you will have paid nearly $500 in interest.

- If you had $2,500 of credit card debt at 17 percent interest, and only made the minimum payment, it would take you 119 months (nearly 10 years) and cost you almost $1,300 in interest.

- If you owed $5,000 at 17 percent interest, and only made the minimum payment, it would take you 145 months (12 years) to pay in full and cost you an additional $2,665 dollars in interest.

These numbers clearly show that making minimum payments on your credit cards costs an enormous amount over the long haul. For this reason, any long-term strategy should focus on getting these debts paid off first and foremost.

After you get your credit cards taken care of, the next step is to order your debts not necessarily by the highest interest rate, but by the longest term—or length—of the debt.

For example, say you have two loans, one with an interest rate of 15 percent and six months left to pay on it, and another with an interest rate of 10 percent and 24 months left to pay. In this case, it's a better long-term decision to concentrate on paying off the 10 percent loan first. This is because over time, that 10 percent loan will cost you more in interest charges than the 15 percent loan will in the next few months.

So organize your debts looking at which one will cost more throughout the life of the debt, and focus on paying those first.

The month-to-month, or cash flow, strategy

This strategy is best suited for those who find it impossible to meet their monthly debt obligations. Since its goal is to reduce the amount paid out in sheer dollars each month, it's a short-term fix for what are likely longer-term financial problems.

It's best to use this strategy only until you can make all of your monthly payments—after that, it's best to switch to a longer-term solution.

The first step is to list all of your monthly bills by ease of payoff. This could mean the smallest amount you owe, or the debt with the shortest time until it's paid in full. To use the two loans in the long-term plan above, you would pay off the 15 percent loan due to end in six months first, then move on to the next.

The advantage to this method is that you can see progress relatively quickly, thus motivating you to stick with the plan. After all, having just one less bill can be like having a huge weight lifted off your shoulders, no matter the size of the bill.

The major disadvantage is that if you have a lot of credit card debt, it usually puts that debt lower on the priority scale, meaning you will pay more in interest over the long run.

If you find yourself consistently using the month-to-month strategy, you may want to consider some type of debt consolidation loan. Doing so can reduce your monthly payments while also paying off longer-term debt (such as credit cards, especially if you only make the minimum payment) in a shorter amount of time.

The interest-rate strategy

This way of prioritizing debt is straightforward: just take all your bills and order them by their interest rate, with the highest as the top priority.

If you use this strategy, remember to use the effective interest rate (EIR). The EIR takes into account any tax deductions you may get on the debt, such as the deduction you receive on mortgage and student loan interest. Since interest payments on these debts are tax deductible—depending on IRS eligibility rules, such as income and the type of residence—the EIR is often lower than whatever is stated on the paperwork.

Other tips

No matter which strategy, or combination of strategies, you use, there are a few more tips you can use, and a few key points to remember:

- **The snowball technique**—Say you have two credit cards, with one bill being $50 a month and another bill $75 a month. Once you pay off the $50 a month card, instead of spending the "extra" $50 you have each month—or, worse yet, taking out another debt that costs the same amount—you instead roll that $50 into paying off the second card. Once that second card is paid off, you then take that $125 and put it toward yet another debt. And so on and so on.

  This is a great method for paying off any type of debt because it doesn't take additional money out of your monthly budget while greatly increasing your chances of paying off a lot of debt relatively quickly.

- **Be flexible**—The nature of military life means things can change quickly, including how much you're paid (due to specialty pays) and the nature of your bills (moving from on-installation housing to off base can lead to a rent payment you didn't have before). So always be ready to adjust to the circumstances, and look to use any extra money you get to pay off debt.

- **Watch for the fees**—Some debts may have a fee for paying the balance in full before the term expires. So before you decide to completely pay off any debt, either check your paperwork or call the creditor to find out if there is an early payoff fee, and what that fee entails.

- **Watch for rate changes**—Some credit cards may have an introductory rate, while your mortgage may be adjustable depending on the prime rate. Take any of these factors into account ahead of time and be prepared for when the rate changes.

- **Control spending**—Part of any plan must also be coupled with a spending plan that keeps you from getting in the same situation. After all, prioritizing and paying off your debt will mean little if you continue to add more debt or spend money unwisely.

- **Make phone calls**—One of the easiest and most effective things you can do is call a creditor before you start having payment problems. They will truly appreciate it, since it shows you care about paying your debt responsibly. It can even lead to solutions you didn't consider, such as a rate reduction or lower payoff amount.

Prioritizing your debt can be difficult, and figuring out which strategy to use in doing so can be complicated, depending on your debt load, income, family situation, and a whole host of other factors.

But it's an essential step in any financial plan and, better yet, can actually make you feel much better about your finances—seeing all your bills and exactly what you owe gives you a sense of control over the situation. And as with any financial plan, the most important thing is follow through. Picking a strategy and organizing bills won't do much if you don't use that strategy effectively and consistently.

So pick your plan, get your debt prioritized, and start down the road toward a secure financial future today!

Credit Protection Plans

There are two schools of thought when it comes to credit protection plans. The first believes consumers should not buy these plans because they benefit the company, not the individual. The other says that these plans serve the public well, providing voluntary credit protection for those that choose it.

In reality, credit protection plans are neither good nor bad—it is the way in which they are sold, and to whom they are sold, that makes all the difference. For the right person, the right plan can be a way to avoid debt after the loss of a loved one, or a lost job, or becoming disabled. For the wrong person it can be a poor financial decision.

Service members and their families need to know the different types of coverage, the limitations of such coverage, and some tips to use when shopping for a plan. Having this knowledge is part of a sound financial strategy, and can help ensure that those defending our country are focused on the job at hand instead of their finances.

What are credit protection plans?

Credit protection plans are sold with credit transactions, such as with loans or credit cards. They are intended to serve as safety nets for consumers by making monthly loan payments when the insured is temporarily disabled or unemployed, or paying off the entire loan balance if the borrower dies. These plans are always optional. If you decide to purchase one, the cost is typically added to your monthly loan payment.

There are four basic types of credit protection plans:

1. **Credit Life**—Pays off the debt if the borrower dies.
2. **Credit Disability**—Pays all or part of a borrower's monthly loan payment should the borrower become disabled.

3. **Involuntary Unemployment Insurance**—Pays all or a part of a borrower's monthly loan payment in the event the borrower loses income as a result of involuntary unemployment.

4. **Credit Property Insurance**—This type of coverage applies to the item(s) offered as collateral while obtaining a loan or other credit product, or that you purchased using credit. This insurance usually does not cover mobile homes or real estate.

Do I need one?

Whether or not you need a credit protection plan depends on a number of different factors. In general, consumers who do not have other insurance coverage, alternate sources of income or savings will find credit protection products useful when paying debts if something unexpected happens. Such coverage can help a family weather a temporary loss of income and avoid other financial problems.

Other times, however, paying for additional coverage may not be in a family's best interest. The California Department of Insurance notes that it will depend on the current level of insurance coverage, the flexibility of that coverage, and future income potential as to whether or not a protection plan is a good financial decision.

The key is to assess your family's own financial situation and coverage before making your decision. Your spouse has life insurance provided through Servicemembers' Group Life Insurance (SGLI) and, while this coverage is often enough, you should ensure that it would cover all current debts. This is vital since your financial obligations do not go away because of death or disability, and many creditors will pursue claims against the estate. You may also want to consider what will happen once your spouse leaves the military and whether or not any other coverage will still be adequate.

Is it optional?

Absolutely. All credit protection plans—credit life, disability, and involuntary unemployment insurance products—are optional and a lender cannot require enrollment as a condition for your being approved for credit.

The one exception may be items used for collateral. Depending on state laws, some lenders may require insurance on the item you use to secure a loan (for example, a car used as collateral on a personal loan). This does not mean, however, that you must purchase the lender's product. Instead, you may provide proof of insurance that lasts throughout the term of the credit transaction.

When buying any credit protection plan, the lender must also include notice of the policy in all of the disclosure documents. The Truth and Lending Act of 1968 requires the creditor to provide a written disclosure of the cost and notification that the purchase is voluntary and not a factor in the decision to extend credit.

Just remember that these plans are all completely optional. So if you feel pressured into purchasing any type of insurance, if the seller is not answering your questions to your satisfaction, or if you have any doubts, do not purchase the coverage.

How much is it?

The cost depends on a number of different factors, including the type of insurance, the lender, and how much coverage you are purchasing. For example, Navy Federal Credit Union offers three different "Payment Protection Plan" options that vary from seven cents per $100 borrowed, to 22 cents per $100, and all have different maximum payout amounts.

Whether or not your family can afford the coverage will depend on how much insurance you already have and how much money you are borrowing. If you have enough current insurance to cover the debt, such additional coverage may not be necessary, but if you would have a problem paying the debt if you or your spouse were injured, then you may want to consider the cost.

Also remember that you are not obligated to purchase any credit insurance product through the lender from whom you are getting the loan. In fact, there are many third-party companies that offer these products, so shop around and make sure your family is getting the best deal.

Military issues

It is important that any policy that covers your spouse has no "acts of war" exclusions. Many policies will not pay out if your spouse dies or is disabled because of an act of war, so read the fine print to make sure you are purchasing appropriate coverage.

Moving around often can also affect how much you initially pay and the limitations offered by a credit protection plan. This is because each state has different rules and maximum allowable rates—some rates can even vary according to the type of lender.

If you buy a policy over the Internet, the laws of the state in which the company operates will dictate the terms of the contract, not necessarily where you live. Make sure to investigate the company and know in which state they do business—the difference between companies can mean the difference of hundreds of dollars for the same amount of coverage.

Helpful tips

Before buying any credit protection plan, you should consider a number of different factors:

- **Know the cost**—Since the cost of a plan can be included in the price of a credit transaction (i.e. added into a personal loan or mortgage), make sure that all fees and costs are disclosed in any paperwork.

- **Know the limitations**—When buying coverage, check for any waiting periods or pre-existing condition requirements.

- **Compare**—There can be differences in the flexibility and cost of the benefits between a credit protection plan and traditional life and disability insurance. Know what each type of policy offers in order to make an informed purchasing decision.

- **Review exclusions**—Make sure that the policy will pay out if your spouse dies or is disabled because of an act of war.

- **Ask questions**—If there is anything about the coverage that you don't understand, keep asking until you completely understand what you are purchasing. If you do not get the answers you want or understand, ask someone else or do not buy the coverage.

- **Find a reputable provider**—Always investigate the company offering you the coverage. Find out how long they've been in business, if they are a member of the Better Business Bureau, and their levels of customer satisfaction.

- **It's always optional**—Remember that lenders cannot condition a consumer loan on whether or not you purchase a credit protection plan. It should always be listed as an optional item.

While some families may never need such plans, for those who live paycheck to paycheck, can't qualify for traditional insurance, and have no savings, a credit protection plan can provide an important safety net.

Dealing with Deployment

With so much going on before, during, and after a military deployment—the preparation, the training, the loving goodbyes and reunions—it is easy to see how seemingly and separately "small" details that go with deployment may slip through the cracks.

Pre-Deployment

Whether administrative, legal or financial, there are a number of tasks families need to complete before the deployment date.

The following tips can help you and your family better prepare for what is a stressful time, and may help mitigate some unnecessary difficulties associated with your spouse's departure and return.

> *Whether administrative, legal or financial, there are a number of tasks families need to complete before deployment.*

There are a number of financial tasks that need to be addressed to help ensure a seamless transition during deployment:

- **Policies and Benefits**—Spend a couple of hours with your spouse going over insurance, investments, benefits, and beneficiaries, as well as the location of the policy documents. Be very clear about what is expected, explain the details, and make sure both of you write down your desires for future reference.

- **Tax-Free and Hazardous-Duty Pay**—Service members may receive several hundred dollars more each month due to hazardous-duty pay, or a tax exemption on wages earned while in a war zone. This is a good opportunity to build up savings or pay off outstanding debt.

Decide as a family what you are willing to commit these funds to before deployment, and then create a plan and follow through with it.

- **Financial Obligations**—Review your monthly budget and contact creditors to ask about paying bills by allotment or Electronic Funds Transfer (EFT). It may be easier to pay bills online rather than by mail. You may also want to consider a debt management loan that can consolidate many bills into just a single payment to be managed during deployment.

- **The Servicemembers' Civil Relief Act (SCRA)**—If a service member's military obligation has affected his or her ability to pay financial obligations such as credit cards, loans, mortgages, etc., the service member can have his or her interest rate capped at six percent for the duration of the active-duty obligation. There are two key parts, however, for you and your spouse to consider:

  o The interest rate reduction only applies to debts incurred *prior* to active duty service, making this almost exclusively apply to those who serve in the National Guard and Reserve and were called up to serve. If your spouse was already on active duty when the financial obligation was taken, then the rate reduction will not apply.

  o The service member must prove that he or she has been materially affected by coming on active duty.

- **Direct Deposit**—If you are keeping the same bank or credit union, direct deposit will not be affected. If you are switching institutions, make sure that the new direct deposit is working correctly before canceling the old bank account. As a rule of thumb, wait at least one month to ensure that everything is working properly.

- **Bills**—Make sure that all bills are organized with a payment plan ready and a power of attorney is in place if needed. Also, be sure to inform creditors, banks and any investment representatives of the deployment.

- **Income Tax**—If you will be deployed when taxes are due, decide in advance how income taxes will be filed. Extensions can be filed through the Internal Revenue Service by filing Form 2350: Application for Extension of Time to File U.S. Income Tax Return, available at www.deploymentlink.osd.mil/pdfs/tax_ext.pdf.

There are also a number of administrative tasks that are simple and straight-forward, but sometimes overlooked during the pre-deployment process:

- **Defense Enrollment Eligibility Reporting System (DEERS)**— Verifying DEERS enrollment prior to deployment will ensure that your family can receive medical care while your spouse is deployed. To confirm enrollment contact DEERS at 1-800-538-9552.

- **ID Cards**—Check the expiration date of all ID cards. If they expire prior to the end of the deployment, contact the appropriate person-nel office to initiate the paperwork.

- **Service Record**—Check for the correct contact information in case of an emergency.

- **Contact List**—Compile a precise list of agencies, businesses, and units that offer assistance in case of an emergency. This is both for your family that's staying stateside and your deployed spouse.

- **Staying in touch with home**—For your spouse, include a voice recorder (tape or digital), stationery, stamps, an address book, and/or e-mail addresses, depending on what is allowed.

- **Red Cross Notifications**—The Red Cross is often the most efficient and rapid way to contact service members overseas. Write down your local Red Cross contact information, including phone number, address and hours. The Red Cross also has an entire section dedicated to help-ing military families on their Web site, www.redcross.org.

- **Spouse Relocation**—It is imperative that command is notified with new contact numbers and addresses if you will be moving to a new location (back to a hometown, closer to family, etc.) during your spouse's deployment. If moving off post, housing authorities will need to be notified in advance of the move. Your creditors should also be notified of your new address so they can send the bills there, helping you to avoid missing a payment.

> *It is imperative that command is notified with new contact information if you will be moving to a new location during your spouse's deployment.*

And finally, there are several legal tasks that are often overlooked:

- Power of Attorney—There are several different types of Powers of Attorney:

  o **General Durable Power of Attorney**—A general grant of authority that authorizes a spouse to act on behalf of the other in financial affairs. It can be revoked at any time and usually takes effect immediately unless otherwise stated in the document.

  o **Health Care Power of Attorney**—This is for when one spouse becomes incapacitated and is unable to make medical decisions on his or her own, as determined by one or more physicians.

  o **Limited Power of Attorney**—This document is intended to grant a spouse a limited amount of authority with regard to one or more matters. For example, it can grant you the authority to make withdrawals from a specific bank account in order to pay bills, but nothing else.

- **Wills**—The military will assist with a General Will and Testament. However, both a Living Will and Ethical Will are also options.

  o In a **Living Will**, either you or your spouse can state wishes regarding future health care in case one or both of you become incapacitated and are unable to share your wishes. This includes how to handle such issues as having a feeding tube inserted or removed, or if "extraordinary" measures should be used.

  o An **Ethical Will** is a letter that expresses feelings on common themes such as personal and spiritual beliefs, values, life's lessons, forgiving or asking for forgiveness, and love. This information is then shared with family and friends in case of death.

- **Servicemembers' Group Life Insurance (SGLI)**—Each active duty service member is eligible for life insurance, which is available in increments of $50,000, up to a maximum of $400,000 (as of 2008; the level can be raised or lowered by Congress). Before deployment, verify beneficiaries and make changes as necessary.

Having all of these housekeeping matters resolved can make what is a time of great anxiety and uncertainty much easier for you and your family. And the effort to organize and manage your legal and financial issues can wind up paying huge dividends during post-deployment as well.

For more information on how the military can help before deployments, visit www.deploymentlink.osd.mil..

During Deployment

Deployments can be a time of great emotional stress, but there is one bright spot: it can give your family a chance to pay off bills and save for the future. This is due to a number of financial incentives, regulations and bonuses paid to those who are deployed.

The following is a list of some, but not all, of the benefits your spouse will earn during his or her deployment. Remember that these can vary depending on your spouse's rank, branch of service, and exactly where he or she is deployed.

- **Basic Allowance for Subsistence (BAS)**—Deploying service members will receive BAS/Separate Rations. It will continue for those who are receiving it at the time of deployment, and it will be started for those who are on meal cards.

- **Per Diem**—All deployed service members who are in a Temporary Change of Station (TCS) or Temporary Duty (TDY) status are entitled to outside the continental United States (OCONUS) incidental per diem. How much and the maximum allowed depends on where he or she is stationed.

- **Hostile Fire Pay (HFP)/Imminent Danger Pay (IDP)**—HFP/IDP is payable to all service members in the total land and air space of a designated Hostile Fire/Imminent Danger area. Service members receive an amount for each month, or part of a month, in which he or she is present in the HFP/IDP area. Entitlement starts upon arrival to the authorized location and terminates upon departure.

- **Combat Zone Tax Exclusion (CZTE)**—Service members in a war zone (however brief, and including airspace) who are on official duty, even for one day, qualify for CZTE for that month. All pay for both enlisted personnel and warrant officers is tax exempt for the months spent in the CZTE area. All enlisted pay, allowances, and leave, earned in a TDY location, designated for CZTE, are tax free.

- **Bonuses**—Paid based on rank when earned, even if paid in installments over the next several years.

- **Leave**—When tax exempt leave is taken, taxable wages are reduced on your spouse's W-2 form, based on the number of days he or she spent on tax-exempt leave.

- **Hardship Duty Pay-Location (HDP-L)**—Indicated as "Save Pay" on your spouse's Leave and Earnings Statement (LES), HDP-L is payable to all service members on a monthly basis according to location and living conditions.

- **Family Separation Allowance (FSA)**—The purpose of Family Separation Allowance (FSA) is to defray minor costs incurred due to enforced separation of more than 30 days. It is paid when a service member is involuntarily separated from his/her dependents or active duty spouse for more than 30 days.

- **Savings Deposit Program (SDP)**—All service members deployed at least 30 consecutive days may contribute to this risk-free program. Your spouse may make any number of deposits in any amount each month, provided the total deposited in a one month period does not exceed his or her monthly net pay and allowances.

  Active duty members may make deposits by cash, personal check, traveler's check, money order or allotment, while reserve component members may make deposits by cash, personal check or money order only. Standing policies regarding personal check acceptance and regulatory restrictions regarding number and type of allotments apply.

  Money cannot be taken out of the account until after your spouse leaves a designated combat zone, except for emergency situations. For more complete information about the SDP and its many requirements and rules, visit www.dfas.mil.

Remember that this is a partial list of benefits your spouse is entitled to when deployed. Not all will apply, and the amounts of each can vary dramatically.

Regardless, all can increase the amount of pay your spouse will receive (or in the case of tax-free pay, reduce the amount of taxable income, which can lead to a nice refund the next year) and give your family a chance to pay off debt and save some money for the future.

Post-deployment

If you planned well before deployment, and paid off debt and saved money during it, then your spouse's homecoming can be a time of great joy, both emotionally and financially.

There are a few things to consider, however, now that the extra money your family received during deployment will no longer be there.

- **Review your financial situation as a couple**—It's vital that both of you sit down and discuss your current financial situation within the first few weeks of your spouse's return. This can help not only with finances, but also with reintegrating your spouse back into "normal" life.

- **Savings Deposit Program (SDP)**—If your spouse took advantage of this program, remember that withdrawals can begin once he or she returns from the designated combat zone, and interest will stop accruing 90 days after he or she returns.

- **Powers of Attorney**—Check the effective dates of these documents, including when they end. If there is still a need for you to have the documents in force, make any changes if necessary.

- **Servicemembers' Civil Relief Act**—If your spouse was called to active duty from the National Guard or Reserve, the interest rate reduction on all debts will end when he or she returns home. Be prepared for this and be sure to budget for the increase in the monthly bill it will bring.

- **Take another look at insurance**—Take another look at any insurance policies you have, including those offered through the military, and readjust the amount of coverage, beneficiaries, etc., as necessary since some information may have changed during deployment.

- **Meet with a financial advisor**—Many military installations, and even a few financial services companies, offer some sort of free financial advice to military families. Use your spouse's homecoming as an opportunity to sit down as a family and reassess where you are financially and where you want to be in the future.

- **Prepare for the next time**—Deployments are part of military life, and just because this one ended doesn't mean another one isn't on the horizon. Take a look at what worked this time, what didn't, and change those things that can make the next deployment easier.

- **Do something nice**—While going on a reckless spending spree is never, ever a good idea, take a look at your family budget and see if there's any money to do a little something special. Perhaps a trip to see family, or even a night just for you and your spouse at a nice restaurant.

Remember that emotions can run high during post-deployment, and it's easy to overdo it financially. Many families go overboard trying to make up for lost time, only to find themselves trapped under a truckload of debt.

The key is to be patient, both emotionally and financially. Give yourself and your partner time to get back into the rhythm of being a family again, and practice patience in easing back into a new financial and family routine.

Perfecting Your PCS

Periodic moves are a basic fact of military life. It is estimated that every year one-third of all military members make Permanent Change of Station (PCS) moves, with an average time of two years between PCS moves. These moves typically involve the members' dependents and household goods.

Since military life can be hectic due to frequent moves, it is vital that you prepare yourself to handle such stress. It is also important that you prepare your finances for the wide range of issues that will inevitably arise.

When PCS orders are received, your family is confronted with many significant changes. But proper planning will help avoid expensive out-of-pocket expenses.

It is estimated that, every year, one-third of all service members PCS, with an average time of two years between moves.

Before the move

Thirty days in advance is a good time to start preparing your house, family and furnishings for the movers. Make sure if there are any changes in orders that you contact the local transportation office.

While the carrier is responsible for packing and preparing your property—they must mark each box with a brief description of content, and provide you an accurate and legible inventory of your household goods—it's also a good idea to do an inventory of your valuable items. Start a spreadsheet that has all your electronics, CDs and DVDs, computer equipment, jewelry, etc., listed by manufacturer, model number, and estimated purchase date and cost. You can even capture it all in video or pictures, just so long as everything is easily identifiable.

If you have recently purchased anything, keep the receipt. This could save you leg work if it is lost or damaged. Put the receipts along with small items and necessities you will carry with you instead of leaving with the movers, like medical and dental records, pictures, etc.

Prior to the movers arriving, you should also do the following:

- Unplug all appliances and electronics.
- Have original boxes near the item if available.
- Dismantle all outdoor equipment.
- Drain water from fridge, washers and other large appliances.
- Drain all fluids from lawn equipment.
- Detach any brackets, curtain rods or storage equipment.
- Take down pictures.
- Remove personal property from the attic, crawl space, etc.
- Remove satellite dish.
- Secure the items that are not being moved to another room and mark them as such.
- Keep an eye on all the packing that goes on to ensure nothing is forgotten.

Watch your weight

The military will use an estimated weight of all your possessions (excluding "professional" materials such as books, papers and equipment for work) to determine its cost. From a fiscal fitness perspective, moving "weight" that exceeds the authorized allowance can cost you out-of-pocket money. These charges could range from several hundred to several thousand dollars. In addition, the charges could come months after your move.

If you receive an overweight notification, check to make sure professional items were credited to your total weight allowance. This should be listed as "Professional Books, Paper and Equipment" (PBP&E).

Keep what you can

Check with your local transportation office, but in many cases you can save a little money by watching what you throw out. While aerosol cans and liquids cannot be moved, spices and canned goods can, which can save you upwards of $100. So if weight is not an issue, you may want to move these to your new home and save some money. And for things that cannot be moved, give them to a friend, or donate them to someone in need.

Entitlement programs

Planning for your move also includes a thorough knowledge of the many entitlements that your family may be able to receive. Some entitlements are applicable only for moves within the U.S., some are for moves outside of the country, and some are for either. While the following can give you an idea of what is available, you should also ask your local finance office for more information.

- **PCS Per Diem Allowance**—Paid to reimburse your family for meals and lodging en route to the new duty station, this amount is the sum total paid per day. There are certain amounts for each family member depending on age, and it can be advanced up to 80 percent of the estimated cost.

- **Dislocation Allowance (DLA)**—This is intended to help with all of those miscellaneous costs of moving, such as connecting utilities, paying deposits, etc. DLA is not normally paid when you initially move. Instead, it is paid when the travel voucher is filed after the move, although you can request an advance.

  DLA is only paid once per fiscal year, even if your family moves multiple times. It is also not usually paid on a local move, or if your spouse is assigned to government quarters at the new duty station and is not accompanied by family members.

- **Monetary Allowance in Lieu of Transportation (MALT)**—This is also known as "mileage" and is intended to offset costs related to driving your vehicle to the new duty station. Paid by travel voucher, MALT may include up to two vehicles, and per mile rates will vary.

- **Mobile Home Transportation**—This applies when a commercial transporter moves a mobile home. Reimbursement includes carrier charges, road fares and tolls, permits and charges for the pilot car. If towed by a private transporter, reimbursement is for actual costs. And for self-propelled mobile homes, reimbursement is at the regular mileage rate.

- **Temporary Lodging Expense (TLE)**—Only paid for moves within the U.S., TLE is intended to help pay the cost of lodging and meals while the family is staying in temporary housing. The ten-day TLE limit can be divided between the last duty station and the new one.

- **Temporary Lodging Allowance (TLA)**—TLA is only paid for moves outside of the U.S., and covers up to 60 days (which can be extended if needed) for temporary lodging and meal expenses after arriving at a new overseas location.

- **Move-In Housing Allowance (MIHA)**—Only for moves outside of the U.S., MIHA is intended to pay for one-time rent related expenses, modification of homes for security reasons, and the initial cost of making a home habitable. MIHA is only available at certain locations.

- **Advance Basic Allowance for Housing (BAH)**—Receiving an advance on BAH requires commander approval, and is generally limited to three months within the U.S., and 12 months overseas. Remember that this is not extra money; it is an advance on the normal BAH and will be deducted from monthly pay.

- **Advance Pay**—If you absolutely need the money, you can get an interest-free advance for up to three months base pay to help with moving. Typically paid back over 12 months, this should only be used in extraordinary circumstances.

It is very important to keep all paperwork pertaining to your move—you may not be eligible for any reimbursements without the proper documentation.

For more PCS information, visit www.defenselink.mil and search for "relocate."

Happier Holidays

Birthdays, graduations, weddings, anniversaries, the holidays ... when it comes to gift giving, military families face the same dilemma as most people: how to pay for it. Many times, when people need extra cash to make ends meet or to pay for unexpected expenses, they turn to payday loans or high-interest credit cards. But with high fees, automatic rollovers, and minimum payments, service members can quickly fall into an endless cycle of debt using these methods of payment.

Every year, millions of Americans quickly discover that all those presents under the tree have led to a mountain of bills in their mailbox. Consumer groups call it the "holiday debt hangover," an affliction that, according to Consumer Reports, caused Americans to incur $63.6 billion in credit card debt alone in 2006.

> *With the average household saddled with $9,000 in debt already, anything that adds to that ... could be devastating.*
> *–Consumer Reports*

For military families, it can be even more difficult due to tighter budgets and lower pay than civilian counterparts. Add in the stress of having loved ones deployed, and the pressure can be difficult to handle for a military spouse.

There is a cure, however, and there are a few things you can do to not only recover from this past holiday season, but also make sure you don't fall victim next year.

Paying off last year

The Web site creditcards.com notes that the average household charged $1,100 in 2006 for holiday gifts. Consumer Reports noted on CNN that "credit cards

can be hazardous to your holiday spending. With the average household sad-
dled with $9,000 in debt already, anything that significantly adds to that …
could be potentially devastating."

One option of paying off that debt is shuffling it from one credit card to
another with a lower rate. But doing so is just a short-term fix—even if you
move the balance to a "low-interest" card, it can still take years to pay in full,
meaning that you could still be paying for last year's presents several years
down the road.

For example, if you had even half the average credit card balance noted by
Consumer Reports—$4,500—at a rate of 15 percent, and you made just the
minimum payment every month (four percent of the balance), it would take
you 134 months (*11 years*) to pay off and you would have to pay nearly $2,000
in interest.

If you moved that balance to a card with an interest rate of only seven percent, it would still take you 111 months (*9 years*) to pay the balance in full.
(Chapter 4: Smart Borrowing, has more information on credit cards.)

One way to pay off debt is get a traditional installment loan like those found
at banks, credit unions, and military loan companies. While the monthly payments may be a bit higher when compared to a minimum credit card payment, it can be a vital part of striking a balance between your monthly budget
(something that is vital on a tight budget) and long-term financial success.
You'll also know exactly when the debt will be paid, something that cannot be
underestimated.

If your credit card debt is significantly smaller, see if there is any way to pay
off the card in full. And if you find yourself between the areas of too much to
pay off at once, yet not enough to justify a loan, try your best to pay more than
the minimum payment. Doing so pays off the principal faster and limits the
amount of interest you are charged.

Preparing for next year

Once you get your past spending taken care of, the next step is to plan ahead for
next year's holiday. There are several ways to do so:

- **Spread out your shopping**—Create a list of everyone who you would
  like to give gifts to throughout the year, including the holidays, and
  then create a budget. Then, keep the list at all times so you can buy
  presents as you find them throughout the year. The goal is to spread
  out the spending over time, instead of suddenly needing several hundred dollars all at once. It can also eliminate impulsive—and often

costly—last-minute decisions, and maintains preparedness for unexpected bargains.

- **Make something**—Have kids make something from the whole family. The gift of food almost always draws rave reviews. The goal here is creativity and cost-effectiveness, as well as a personal touch that makes the gift much more special.

- **Consider a group gift**—If family members and others will be purchasing a gift for the same person, consider pooling money to buy a single gift. A small contribution from several people is transformed into a larger gift when leveraging buying power.

- **Do something special**—Offer to spend time with a recipient in a way that is meaningful. For a child, that might be helping build a snow fort after the first snow or spending the afternoon at the movies or in the park. For a grandparent, it might be helping with repairs around the house or planting flowers in the yard. A coupon for free "babysitting" is always a welcomed gift for parents that cannot otherwise get away. Again, creativity is the most important thing.

- **Make a donation to charity**—For those who seem to have everything, giving them one more "thing" won't mean much. But making any size donation to their favorite charity in their name would be a special way to honor them. As a bonus, you may also get a tax deduction.

While these tips can be helpful, they won't mean much without financial discipline. So maintain the budget you drew up, avoid those last-minute decisions, and find creative solutions for sometimes-difficult problems. If you do, it'll make the holiday celebrations that much more sweet.

Buying a Car

Buying a new car can often be a stressful and expensive experience. But if you take a few important steps you will not only save yourself some headaches, you can also save yourself thousands of dollars. The following are some basic tips that can make the process easier on your nerves and wallet, broken down into three different sections.

Get your finances in order

If you take a few important steps you will not only save yourself some headaches, you can also save yourself thousands of dollars.

These first two steps should be done before anything else.

- **Get a copy of your credit report**—Knowing your credit score and if you have any blemishes on your report will have huge impacts on your financing and payments. So if you haven't yet received a free copy of your report in the past year, visit www.annualcreditreport.com (the only site officially designated to do so) and get yours from all three bureaus. (For more information on credit reports, see Chapter 2: The Importance of Your Credit Report.)

- **Get your financing in order**—Unless you have enough cash stashed under your mattress, you will need to borrow money in order to get that new or used car. Make a budget, find out how much you can afford in monthly payments and then get financing. Whether you are buying from a dealer or an individual, receiving financing beforehand from a bank, credit union or reputable loan company means that you have a set amount and can negotiate on your terms.

Do some research

- **Assess what you actually need**—Some people buy a car because it looks cool, is the newest trend, or is the one they have always wanted. It doesn't take long before they learn the car is impractical, gets horrible gas mileage or is too expensive to maintain. A car should reflect your personality, but you should not sacrifice your budget or get into overwhelming debt.

- **Focus on reliability**—It is vital that you have a car that isn't going to break down when your spouse needs to get back to base. Magazines such as Consumer Reports, sites such as consumerguide.com, and several other sources offer impartial research on repair costs, quality of construction, gas mileage and other important items.

- **Narrow your choices**—Select two or three models that you want, and then take the next two steps to make your decision:

  - **Look at insurance costs**—Contact at least three different insurance companies to find out how much it will cost to insure your new (or used) automobile. Ask how much the difference in cost will be with a change in deductibles; there can be a large difference in cost if you have a $1,000 deductible compared to $500. You can also go to a company such as Progressive Auto Insurance. They will give you free quotes from up to four companies and let you know how much it will cost each month.

  - **Comparison shop**—If you are buying a new car, you can visit a dealer's website, look at costs at dealers from another town or city, or even buy straight from the factory. If you are buying a used car, the standard is usually Kelly Blue Book, but you should use more than one publication or website, such as Edmunds Auto or the National Automobile Dealers Association (NADA) to find a consensus price on a used car.

Take action

Now that you have your financing in order, have done your research and have an idea of what it will cost to pay for and insure your new car, it is time to go and get it.

- **Trade-in**—If you plan on trading in your old car, do not wait until it is ready to head to the junk yard—it can (and should) take several months to research, obtain financing and decide on what car you should buy. Waiting until the last minute can force you into a hasty, ill-informed and desperate decision.

- **Skip the extras**—The easiest way to save money is to avoid all of the extras offered by dealers like undercoating, rust protection and extended warranties. You can buy extended warranties on the Internet for a fraction of the cost, and the extra sprays and fabric protectants do little, if anything, to truly help your car last longer.

- **Buying a used car**—Never buy a used car without a report from CARFAX, the standard for information on used cars. By running a vehicle history report you can see if the car was totaled, salvaged, rebuilt, flooded, failed inspection, stolen ... basically, you can find out pretty much everything you want to know about the car you are looking at buying. And if you know a reputable mechanic, ask to have him or her look at the car—they can often identify any problems that are not on the CARFAX report.

  If you are buying used from a dealer, never, ever sign an "As Is" paper. Always get at least a 30-day warranty or, if possible, a 90-day guarantee. Many states have "lemon laws," but there are still a few questionable salespeople who may try to pass their problem car on to you.

Now that you've prepared yourself and done the necessary research, odds are you will get a quality vehicle at a quality price. And if you make sure to change the oil, properly inflate and rotate the tires, and drive safely, you will have reliable transportation you can enjoy for a number of years.

Simple Tax Tips

Few people enjoy doing or even thinking about their taxes—the rules and regulations are often confusing, discovering what is and is not deductible can take weeks, and seeing how much of your money is taken each year can be disheartening.

But diligence and knowledge of the latest tax information have many benefits, including decreasing the likelihood of errors on your return, lessoning the chance that you'll require a filing extension (thus incurring penalties), allowing you to receive your refund check more quickly, and easing overall stress associated with this mundane task.

To help guide you through this process, the following tax tips and savings advice can make things a bit easier for you and your family.

Know important dates

While the typical due date is April 15 of each year, it can be extended if the day falls on a weekend. Waiting until the last minute, however, can cost you in several ways.

First, many tax preparers charge more as the deadline gets closer. Second, you may not have time to find all of the deductions to which you are entitled, causing you to pay more or receive less in a refund. And third, the IRS is typically swamped, meaning your refund can take longer to get back to you (if you're getting a refund).

If your spouse is deployed to a combat zone, the IRS automatically extends the deadline several months for filing your tax return—but only if you are filing jointly.

Since most people have all of their required forms by early February, the best idea is to get your taxes done as early as possible.

Filing Extensions

If your spouse is deployed to a combat zone, the IRS automatically extends the deadline several months for filing your tax return—but only if you are filing jointly. If you are filing separately, then yours will still be due on April 15 (or thereabouts) while your deployed spouse will get the extension. The deadline is also extended for service members deployed overseas away from their permanent duty station in a qualified hazardous duty area.

Get organized

Whether you're preparing your own return or hiring a professional, you'll need to organize your receipts and records to make the process run as smoothly as possible. Some of the documents and information you need include:

- W-2, W-2G and 1099 forms.
- Mortgage interest documents.
- Medical expense receipts.
- Charitable contribution receipts.
- Daycare receipts.
- Thrift Savings Plan contribution records.
- IRA contribution records.
- State and local general sales tax receipts.
- Receipts for higher education expenses.

Understand your tax breaks

As the spouse of a service member, you and your family are eligible for several tax benefits. The Military Family Tax Relief Act and a number of other laws allow certain benefits and gains to be excluded from income on your federal tax return. And of course, reporting a lower income reduces the amount of taxes you are required to pay the federal government.

- **Home sales**—If you have a gain from the sale or exchange of your home, you may be able to exclude all or part of the gain from your income. To be eligible, you must own your home and have used it as your primary residence for two out of the last five years before the sale.

However, if your spouse was on "qualified extended duty," you may extend the ownership period for up to 10 years. You are on qualified extended duty when you are at a duty station that is at least 50 miles from the residence sold, or residing under orders in government housing for more than 90 days.

- **Overnight travel expenses**—Guard and reservists who stay overnight more than 100 miles away from home while in service may deduct unreimbursed travel expenses (e.g. transportation, meals and lodging).

- **Combat Zone Extensions Expanded to Contingency Operations**—The same extensions granted to combat zone participants to file returns or pay taxes will also apply to those serving in Contingency Operations, as designated by the Secretary of Defense.

- **Death benefits**—For deaths occurring after Sept. 10, 2001, a new law doubles the tax-free, lump-sum benefit paid to survivors of deceased Armed Forces members from $6,000 to $12,000. (Note: The amount could change again in the future.)

- **Department of Defense Homeowners Assistance Program**—Under this program, payments made after Nov. 11, 2003, to offset the adverse effects on housing values due to military base realignments or closures can be excluded from income as a fringe benefit.

- **Dependent Care Assistance Program**—Dependent care assistance programs for military families are excludable from income.

- **Earned Income Tax Credit (EITC)**—Service members have the option of treating excludable combat pay (but not the basic allowance for housing or basic allowance for subsistence) as earned income for purposes of the EITC. This could help avoid a situation in which your spouse's military pay exclusion leads to no earned income and, thus, no EITC.

Under this provision, military personnel may opt to include all or none of their combat pay—but not just part of it—when calculating their EITC. If you use the IRS' "Free File," the program will automatically calculate the EITC for you.

Retirement Plan Considerations

If your spouse is serving in a designated combat zone, he or she can now put the money into an individual retirement account (IRA), even though the income is tax-free—previously, there was a minimum amount of taxable income required to contribute to such plans. Congress changed this in 2006 with the Heroes Earned Retirement Opportunities (HERO) Act.

The HERO Act allows service members to count tax-free combat pay when determining whether they qualify to contribute to a qualified retirement plan. Before this change, members of the military whose earnings came entirely from tax-free combat pay were generally discouraged from using IRAs to save for retirement, since they did not have enough taxable income and due to the large tax bill associated with contributing to such plans.

Also, as the IRS Web site notes:

> *Taxpayers choosing to put money into a Roth IRA don't need to report these contributions on their individual tax return. Roth contributions are not deductible, but distributions, usually after retirement, are normally tax-free. Income limits and other special rules apply.*
>
> *On the other hand, contributions to a traditional IRA are often, though not always, deductible, and distributions are generally taxable.*

Contributions to any IRA must be recorded for the year in which they were made, and there are limits on how much money can be put into such accounts.

Note that an IRA is different than the Thrift Savings Plan (TSP) offered through the military—each has different rules and requirements, so contact a tax professional for more information on the tax implications for each.

Utilize free help

As a military spouse, you may be eligible to receive free assistance with the preparation and filing of your federal tax return. The U.S. Armed Forces participates in the Volunteer Income Tax Assistance (VITA) Program. The Armed Forces Tax Council (AFTC) oversees the operation of the military tax programs worldwide, and serves as the main conduit for outreach by the IRS to service members and their families.

The military-based VITA sites provide free tax advice, tax preparation, return filing and other tax assistance. These certified community volunteers are trained by the IRS to address military-specific tax issues, such as combat zone tax benefits, and the services are free for service members and their families.

Consider filing online

Free File allows service members to prepare and electronically file their federal income tax return online. Offered only through the IRS Web site, Free File is available in English and Spanish, and can be accessed from any computer connected to the Internet, making it especially convenient for those stationed abroad. It can also be accessed 24 hours a day, seven days a week.

Another benefit of using Free File is that refunds come faster—usually in half the time. If you use Free File and choose to receive your refund with Direct Deposit, you will receive your refund in as little as 10 days.

For more information on tax saving tips for the military, visit the IRS Web site at www.irs.gov.

The information given in this chapter is for educational purposes only. You should always check with your tax representative or refer to the IRS Web site before filing your income taxes.

Preparing for Financial Emergencies

A young service member paid off several of her credit cards and started putting money away toward emergency savings. Six months later, after having put away $100 a month in an emergency savings fund, the service member was able to withdraw the money she needed to fly home to Idaho when her father unexpectedly had a stroke. Instead of having to "beg, borrow, and plead" to get the money, she had the available funds right there, was able to purchase the tickets online that night and fly out two days later.

One of the most important steps for financial independence is being prepared for unexpected bills. And the best way to do that is to create an Emergency Savings Account (ESA). This is important because it prevents you from having to finance car repairs, a trip home to see family, or other expenses.

With adequate emergency savings, you can focus on how to best meet your family's needs, rather than worrying about finding the money to handle difficult situations.

The need for an ESA

In a survey of active-duty military personnel by the Rand Institute, military families were asked if they had any financial difficulties within the last year. Some of the questions included whether or not they had bounced a check, fell behind on their bills, had to borrow money from family or friends to help make ends meet, or even if they had their car repossessed. More than half of the junior enlisted ranks (E1 to E4) reported having one or more of these difficulties. Noncommissioned officers (E5 and E6) also had experienced such problems, with 40 percent saying they had encountered difficult financial situations.

Most of these money woes could have been easily avoided, however, by having an ESA.

Determine the amount of your ESA

Deciding how much to set aside is unique to each family—there is no hard and fast rule to determine how much is needed. Some experts have recommended a flat $500, while others have recommended three to six months living expenses. Regardless of what you choose, the point is to be able to pay for all of your family's bills for at least two months should all sources of income become unavailable.

One of the few rules that everyone agrees on is to "pay yourself first." This means savings comes first, before the nonessentials are bought and before the vacation is planned. But where do you find the money? Where are the hidden savings?

There are a few tips that can save you money almost every day:

- Save on groceries by planning and clipping coupons; it can save you $250 a year.
- A "change jar" can easily net $100 or more each year.
- Pay cash whenever possible to save yourself thousands in interest.
- Increase insurance deductibles and potentially save hundreds of dollars each year.
- Eliminating two fast food meals per week can save more than $500 each year.
- Deposit your spouse's reenlistment bonus in your ESA, thus building it quickly.

These tips are only the beginning—there are many ways to save enough money to prepare for your financial future, so think of creative ways to find extra money each month. And when you add all those up, you can easily have anywhere from $500 to two month's salary set aside relatively quickly, letting you move on to your mid- and long-range financial goals.

Deciding on the type of account

Your ESA should:

- Be readily available
- Pay you interest
- Have no penalty for withdrawal (including early withdrawal for some accounts)
- Be insured or guaranteed

This can include savings accounts, money market accounts, or money market mutual funds. Remember that while Treasury bills and Certificates of Deposit are relatively safe and secure options, they take longer to access and you may not get their full benefit (i.e. interest) if you withdraw money before they mature.

No matter what type of account you choose, consider having your spouse make the deposit via allotment. Doing so makes the deposit automatic and is a key part of the "pay yourself first" philosophy.

With adequate emergency savings, you can focus on how to best meet your family's needs, rather than worrying about finding the money to handle difficult financial situations. Once an ESA is established, your family can apply those same savings habits toward longer term investments or Thrift Savings Plans, and start down the road to financial success.

Saving For Retirement

There are many ways to have income after retirement: Social Security, interest from investments, and a pension are just a few. For service members, one of the easiest ways to have a secure financial future is to start saving for retirement early by investing in the Thrift Savings Plan (TSP).

TSP Basics

The TSP is a federally-sponsored retirement savings and investment plan that allows military families to set aside money pre-tax, which is similar to a 401(k) plan in the civilian sector. As a "defined contribution" plan, the retirement income received from a TSP account will depend on how much your spouse contributes and the earnings on those contributions.

Putting money in

While your spouse can contribute from one to 100 percent of any pay (except housing, food, etc.) into his or her TSP, the IRS does have limits on how much can be contributed each year.

Contributions are made by allotment and, since they are taken out before taxes are deducted, can actually reduce the total amount of tax your spouse pays.

Taking money out

There are many ways to get money out of a TSP account, and the tax laws regarding such withdrawals can be quite complex. But there are three common ways to take money out before retirement, and each one has its own financial consequences.

- **Transfer**—When your spouse leaves military service, he can simply transfer the money to a civilian employer's qualified retirement plan, into an Individual Retirement Account (IRA), or leave it in the TSP (as long as he starts withdrawing the money by age 70 1/2).

- **Loan**—Your spouse can take out a loan against a TSP account, but there are some guidelines to consider, fees to pay, and tax considerations. Doing so should also be a last resort, since the goal of a TSP account is save for the long haul. For complete TSP information, visit www.tsp.gov.

- **Withdrawals**—Withdrawing money from an account before retirement can be done, but there are a number of factors to consider.

  First, the money withdrawn is taxed immediately, thus eliminating the tax-free savings. Secondly, there is a 10 percent penalty for taking the money early. Both of these can have a dramatic impact on the amount of money received when making an early withdrawal.

  You must also remember that the money cannot be replaced. The TSP Web site states, "When you make an in-service withdrawal, you are removing money from your account forever. It cannot be put back or repaid to your account." The site also points out that if "you make a financial hardship in-service withdrawal, the overall impact can be even greater because you cannot contribute to the TSP for six months following your withdrawal."

Start early, save often

While it's never too late to start a retirement or savings plan, the earlier you start, the better. The reason for this is the power of "compound interest." Compound interest is when the interest earned in an investment is put back into that investment. This way, the interest is itself earning interest and increasing your savings quickly.

As the figures show, compounding interest can grow relatively quickly. And just a few years can mean all the difference between retiring somewhat secure, or retiring as a millionaire.

For an example of the power of compounding interest, take the following chart. It shows the difference in starting a retirement plan at different ages, the amount set aside each month, the total contributed over the course of the account, and the total value of the account by age 65. The rate of return is 10 percent, which is the average annual increase in the stock market for the past 100 years:

Age	Monthly allotment	Total saved	TSP value
35	$50	$18,600	$110,213
25	$50	$24,600	$295,426
18	$50	$28,800	$581,395

As you can see, and as we also highlighted in "Chapter 1: Everyday Spending," starting even a few years earlier can make a dramatic difference in how much you and your spouse will have in retirement. The difference is even more dramatic if the amount is increased to $100 per month:

Age	Monthly allotment	Total saved	TSP value
35	$100	$37,200	$220,426
25	$100	$49,200	$590,854
18	$100	$57,600	$1,100,000

As the figures show, compounding interest can grow relatively quickly. And just a few years can mean all the difference between retiring somewhat secure, or retiring as a millionaire.

How to enroll

The Defense Finance and Accounting Web site has a section where service members can sign up and select TSP contribution amounts. For more information visit www.dod.mil/dfas or www.tsp.gov. Military families can also test TSP planning with many financial calculators on the Internet, as well as on the TSP Web site previously mentioned.

Also, remember that all of the services have formal programs to help families successfully transition from military service to the civilian sector. These programs are available at every installation, staffed with experienced career counselors, and have resources to help plan the transition from active-duty to retired status. Every retiring service member can benefit from these services.

Teaching Kids Money Management

Understanding the concept of money doesn't come naturally to a child, and many schools don't teach basic personal finance. So it's up to you, the parent, to find ways to teach your kids about money that are positive and effective.

While thousands of words have been written on the subject, there are some simple and easy-to-follow dos and don'ts to help children grasp the idea of money.

By interacting with your children and teaching them a positive, effective, and successful attitude toward money, you can create a fun and interesting environment that can prevent problems in the future.

Dos

- **Give your child an allowance**—The key to an allowance is to give your children the chance to make choices regarding money. Deciding how much and how often they receive an allowance will depend on their age and how much you are willing to spend. Also, remember that an allowance is a tool to teach children about money management, not about chores—those should be considered a family responsibility. If you choose to pay them for doing tasks outside of what is normally expected, then consider the task as a way to earn extra funds in addition to the allowance.

- **Educate your child on the different forms money can take**—Look inside your wallet and you'll find a variety of options: coins, dollars, debit cards, credit cards and checks. Eventually, your children will ask about these, so be prepared to tell them how these forms of payment work.

- **Encourage teenagers to get part-time jobs**—Earning money is the best way to teach its value, and it introduces kids to the "real world" of adulthood. They can also use the money to buy a car, pay for insurance, or even to save for college.

- **Stress savings**—Most financial experts recommend that children set aside 10 percent of their allowance into savings. As a way to teach them how a retirement account works, tell them that you'll add money to whatever they put into savings the way companies "match" money put into a retirement account. This can encourage saving money, the savings will grow faster, and children can learn how quickly a little money can add up. Once your children have accumulated enough, open a savings account to teach the concept of interest.

- **Remember to let your children learn on their own time**—Concentrate on guiding your children's attitudes and knowledge about money, not pressuring them. The positive habits you instill now can stick with your children for the rest of their lives.

Don'ts

- **Don't wait to teach your children about money**—Research shows that the sooner children learn how to budget and save, the more likely they will retain those habits into adulthood. Knowing the value of something and how that will affect other purchases is a lesson some adults don't even understand.

- **Don't control the process in the hope they will never make mistakes**—There will be errors, bad purchases, and questionable choices, but that's part of the learning process. It's much better to get them out of the way now with a new bicycle, rather than later in life with a new house.

- **Don't stick to the same allowance for years**—As your children get older, their tastes in clothes and music, and the desire to hang out with friends will all become more expensive. Have a "review" every year (perhaps on their birthdays so it's easy to remember) that allows them to negotiate a higher rate. Just make sure to keep any increase within your family budget.

- **Don't let them get a credit card before they are ready**—Handling a credit card is best left for those children who have shown they are responsible with their finances. Getting a pre-paid debit card can be a good way to teach kids that credit has limits, but without the interest and fees. Only when they show they can use money wisely should they get a credit card.

- **Don't tell your child you don't have the money for something they want**—This can cause a negative (or even spiteful) attitude toward money. Instead, say that the item has to be added to the budget, and money may need to be saved to buy it. This introduces them to a budget and avoids the "gotta have it now" mentality.

Through all of these steps, remember one important thing: Have fun! Money can sometimes be a sore subject, especially when there doesn't seem to be enough of it to go around. But by interacting with your children and teaching them a positive, effective, and successful attitude toward money, you can create a fun and interesting environment that can prevent problems in the future. And as a bonus, you may also learn a little something about yourself in the process.

College Savings 101

Even if you're still buying diapers and baby formula for your child, the thought of sending your little one off to college has probably crossed your mind at some point. It may also cause you some stress since, according to www.collegeboard.com, annual tuition can range between $5,000 a year for a public four-year university, to more than $20,000 for a private college.

But before deciding how—or even if—you're going to help pay for those costs, it's good to look at the numerous ways to pay for college. From tax-deferred savings plans, to grants, to scholarships, there are many different ways to pay for college without saddling yourself with a mountain of debt.

> *Annual tuition can range between $5,000 a year for a public four-year university, to more than $20,000 for a private college.*

Start early with a 529 Plan

A 529 Plan is named after the section of the federal tax code that covers such deductions and allows you to save pre-tax money to pay for college tuition. This money is, in turn, put into some type of investment that earns interest, allowing your money to grow.

Every state has at least one version of a 529 Plan, and all of them have features that make them a great savings tool:

- The money you invest is set aside tax free.
- You can withdraw money from the fund for qualified education expenses, also tax free.

- You take advantage of compounded interest, giving you more money in the long run.

Different types

There are two basic 529 plans, but some states (such as Arizona) offer as many as four varieties. Each of these offers different benefits, restrictions and methods of paying for college.

Prepaid Tuition Plans

These plans allow you to save for a college or university in a specific state. The advantage is that the cost of tuition is locked into the rate charged when you open the plan. With tuition costs continuing to rise, this is a good way to hedge against those raises. The money is also transferable to another family member without tax penalties if your child decides to not attend college.

The disadvantage of the prepaid tuition plan is that most of the states have some type of residency requirement—either you or the child for whom you are saving must be a state resident. If the state does not have a residency requirement, then you might not be eligible for a break on state taxes. This can be quite difficult for military families due to frequent moves and the generally mobile military lifestyle.

To determine your "state of residence" (which may not be where your family is currently stationed), check which state you selected on DD Form 2058 (State of Legal Residence Certificate) or check on your spouse's LES (Leave Earnings Statement).

College Savings Plan

These plans differ from prepaid plans in a number of ways, chiefly in that they accrue much like a retirement savings plan—the money you contribute is invested in mutual funds and can increase as the stock market increases. Since this is a long-term savings plan, the chances of it increasing in value are very good because it won't be affected by temporary fluctuations in the market.

The advantage to this type of plan is that you can use it for higher education in any state. Most have no residency requirement—if you lived in Georgia, you could contribute to a plan in Michigan and send your kids to school in Oregon. However, there are a few states (such as South Dakota) that require residency in all cases. Another advantage is that you can use the money for your own education, or even your spouse's.

The disadvantage is that, if you choose to use an out-of-state plan, you may not receive the full tax advantages offered by an in-state plan. Also, the state or federal government does not insure your 529 investments in any way, so be aware that there is a possibility of the fund losing money.

Similar traits

All 529 plans have a few things in common:

- **Beneficiaries**—The College Savings Plan Networks notes that "anyone can be named the beneficiary of a 529 account, regardless of their relationship to the person who establishes the account. You can even establish an account with yourself as the named beneficiary." This allows you to save for anyone at any time, just so long as he or she is "a U.S. citizen or a resident alien" and "have a social security number or federal tax identification number." You can also have multiple 529 accounts for a single person.

  If your child decides to not attend college, you can change the beneficiary and transfer the funds, so long as it is transferred to a family member. You can also withdraw the money for non-education purposes, but any earnings will be taxed, and some plans have penalties for doing so.

- **Contributors**—Anyone can contribute to a 529 plan; grandparents, cousins, friends, even companies and non-profits. This can lead to many opportunities to save, since so many different people can make a donation.

  > *Anyone can contribute to a 529 plan; friends, grandparents, cousins, even companies and non-profits.*

- **Tax implications**—Contributions are not tax deductible, but you will not be taxed when you withdraw the money for educational costs, and there are no taxes on money earned through the investments in the plan.

To find a listing of the 529 plans offered where you live, and more detailed information, visit www.collegesavings.org, or www.savingsforcollege.com; both have a state-by-state listing of the plans available.

Scholarships can be plentiful

While you or your child may be able to get traditional athletic or academic scholarships, there are literally thousands of scholarships available just for military families. Private and public companies, non-profits, and even the Department of Defense offer scholarships for service members, their spouses, and their children. Even students that have lower grade point averages or test scores may qualify for scholarships that encourage them to continue their education beyond high school.

Where to start

The first and perhaps easiest place to find scholarships is the Internet. A simple Google search can yield more results than you can realistically sort through, so try to be as specific as possible with your terms. For example, searching for "scholarships for daughters of U.S. Army officers in Texas" is more likely to generate useable results than just searching for "scholarships for U.S. Army." Take your time, make a thorough search, and be sure to bookmark any sites that fit your needs.

You can also go through the appropriate military relief agency, military non-profit (i.e. AUSA) and even the commissary system, which has one of the most popular scholarship programs (found at www.militaryscholar.org).

Tips on applying

Every scholarship will have different criteria, whether it be branch of service and school, race, gender or nationality. Some scholarships will have incredibly specific criteria, while others have more general rules. The key is to double check all of the criteria and know the exact requirements—the last thing you want to do is spend time filling out an application and collecting paperwork, only to find your child doesn't qualify.

It is also important to apply for as many scholarships as you can (keeping the criteria in mind) to ensure you're getting as much as you can. Again, though, make sure to read the fine print carefully to ensure there are no rules that may limit your access to other scholarships. For example, one may have some sort of requirement about only paying for room and board, yet you already have that covered with another scholarship.

Whether your or your child's entire schooling is paid for through scholarships, or if you're just applying for a few hundred dollars, it's worth the effort if it can save you money.

Federal financial aid

The federal budget always includes several billion dollars in financial assistance. To receive it, however, you must first carefully complete the Free Application for Federal Student Aid (FAFSA) form and include all the required information. Students can pick up a copy of the FAFSA form from a high school counseling office, or a college financial aid office. You can also download it, or even complete it online, at www.fafsa.ed.gov.

Because financial aid is distributed on a first-come, first-served basis, it is critical you submit the form as soon as possible after January 1, during your child's senior year in high school. Once your student's FAFSA form is reviewed, he or she will be sent a Student Aid Report that outlines the types of government financial aid available based on the information submitted.

To find complete information about the federal financial aid process, visit www.students.gov.

Other places to look

If you decide to apply for financial aid, start by paying a visit to your child's high school guidance counselor. He or she will have a current listing of available scholarships and grants. These professionals are experts in the college application process and can provide assistance with the application. If necessary, he or she can also review essays and provide computer time. Be sure to check back with the counselor often, as updates to available scholarships are frequent.

Visit a college financial aid office, even if it is not your student's college destination. College financial aid offices can be a great help in finding the best financial aid. In addition, various workplaces, civic clubs, not-for-profits and other organizations may offer money for college as well, so do some investigating.

Remember that there are many untapped scholarship and grant dollars for those willing to do the research. And with the rising costs of college tuition, every dollar counts.

Scholarships and aid resources on the Web

There are many sites that can help you track down money to help pay for a college education.

- **www.students.gov**—A portal into federal dollars for education, information about employment, and other issues concerning students.
- **www.pueblo.gsa.gov**—Helpful information about 529 plans.

- **www.collegboard.com**—General information about college costs.
- **www.salliemae.com**—The largest provider of student loans in the country.

The Danger of Identity Theft

Identity theft is America's fastest growing crime. According to the Better Business Bureau (BBB) and the most recently-available statistics, 8.9 million Americans had their identities stolen in 2006 at a cost of $56.6 billion, up from $54.4 billion in 2005.

As more and more information about you circulates on the Internet, the more likely you are to fall prey to those who will use your information to ruin your credit.

An Identity Theft Resource Center (ITRC) study shows:

- Victims spend an average of 600 hours recovering from this crime, often over a period of years. Based on 600 hours times the indicated victim's wages, this equals nearly $16,000 in lost potential or realized income.

- Business community losses average from $40,000 to $92,000 per individual case in fraudulent charges.

- Victims spend an average of $1,400 in out-of-pocket expenses trying to solve the problem.

- 98 million American adults have no idea what to do if identity theft strikes them—and no way of knowing when it's over.

The following chart from the Federal Trade Commission shows just how quickly this crime has grown.

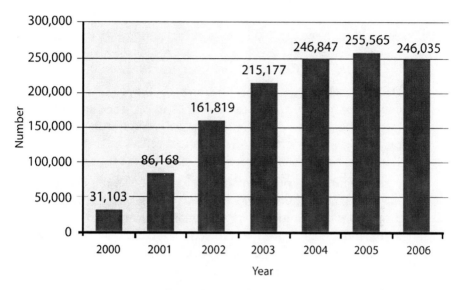

Source: Federal Trade Commission

These statistics show that identity theft not only ruins a person's credit rating, it also costs millions of dollars in lost wages, legal fees and other associated costs. For service members, it can lead to denial of security clearances and even a decline in operation readiness—the men and women in the Armed Forces should be focusing on the job at hand, rather than on financial worries.

And as more and more information about you circulates on the Internet, the more likely you are to fall prey to those who will use your information to ruin your credit.

There are some important things you can do, however, to protect yourself.

- **Avoid giving out your Social Security number**—Once used as a quick and easy way to assign unique identification numbers for health care, business transactions and even driver's licenses, Social Security numbers are the main weapon in the identity thieves arsenal. All a person needs in addition to this is a birth date, address and phone number, and they can ring up an enormous amount of debt in a short time.

There will be some legitimate needs for you to share this information, but only do it if you are sure the company is reputable, and only if you initiated the contact. For items such as driver's licenses or health care, ask if they can use another number instead.

- **Order a credit report at least once a year**—Knowing what is on your credit report can help you catch a problem early and stop the crime from spiraling out of control. The earlier you catch the problem, the easier it will be to correct it. (See Chapter 2: The Importance of Your Credit Report, for more information.)

- **Understand the protections that exist**—In 2003, the new Fair and Accurate Credit Transactions Act (FACTA) was written to offer new protections against identity theft. Detailed information on this legislation and specific consumer protections it contains can be viewed at www.fdic.gov/consumers/consumer/alerts/facta.html.

- **Keep an eye on unused accounts**—Identity thieves will look for dormant accounts, but your credit score is based on how much credit you're using compared to how much you have available. It's a balancing act between protecting yourself and having a good score, so keep your older, higher-limit accounts open, and close smaller and more recent accounts. Keep a close eye on those you don't use as much, and report any suspicious activity immediately.

If you are careful about sharing your personal information, take the time to review your credit report, and document your credit transactions thoroughly, you should be able to limit your risk.

What to do if you're a victim of identify theft

If you find yourself a victim (or have already been one), then contact your local police. They can tell you how to resolve the problem and how to restore your credit, thus giving you the peace of mind you need to perform your duties. Be prepared to provide them with as much information and documentation as possible. Be sure to get a copy of the police report as credit card companies, banks and credit reporting agencies may require you to show a police report to support your claim that a crime was committed.

In addition, report the crime to the Federal Trade Commission (FTC). The federal agency collects complaints about identity theft from consumers and stores them in a secure online database called the Consumer Sentinel that is available to law enforcement agencies worldwide. The FTC can also provide additional information on what you need to do as a victim of identify theft. You can contact the FTC's Consumer Response Center at www.consumer.gov/idtheft/.

Finally, you'll want to contact the fraud units of the three credit reporting agencies: Equifax, Experian and Trans Union. You'll need to ask them to place a fraud alert on your credit report to help prevent new fraudulent accounts from being opened. In addition, as a victim of identify theft, these agencies are required to provide you with a free copy of your credit report every three months, allowing you to further monitor for illegal activity.

Equifax
1-800-685-1111
Credit Information Services
PO Box 740241
Atlanta, GA 30374
www.equifax.com

Experian
1-888-397-3742
National Consumer Assistance Center
PO Box 2104
Allen, TX 75013
www.experian.com

Trans Union
1-800-888-4213
Consumer Disclosure Center
PO Box 1000
Chester, PA 19022
www.transunion.com

Gone Phishing:
How to Avoid Online Scams

Imagine your spouse has served more than 20 years in the military, received numerous commendations, and has built up a level of trust with his peers. He has become everything he wanted to be—perhaps even a bit more—and met every challenge head on and with success.

Then, someone steals his identity. The thief uses it for profit while devastating your family's finances. And they're doing it under his name.

It's called "identity theft," and it happens every day to individuals throughout the military and civilian communities.

For companies, "phishing" is similar to identity theft. The difference is that a phishing scam doesn't seek to rip off a company, but instead uses the good reputation and name of a company to rip off consumers. These scams are dangerous, not always easy to identify, and even the most intelligent and cautious consumers can fall victim.

The way it works

Phishing is a way to get people to share vital financial information, whether via e-mail or over the phone.

Phishers have used phone calls to try and defraud military families—the caller says he or she is from the Red Cross, that the service member has been injured, and the caller needs

For companies, "phishing" is similar to identity theft. The difference is that a phishing scam doesn't seek to rip off a company, but instead uses the good reputation and name of a company to rip off consumers.

personal information. A few families have complied, only to discover their loved one is fine, while his or her bank account is not.

With e-mail, phishers use a real logo, and the e-mail address appears as if it's from a legitimate and well-known company. E-bay, PayPal, Amazon ... all have had, and continue to have, their name used by phishers. Even the Better Business Bureau (BBB) has had its brand stolen and used in phishing scams.

No matter the method, phishing is costing consumers and companies millions of dollars each year.

A company's perspective

A company's "brand" is more than just its logo. It includes position in the market (McDonalds or Wal-Mart), reputation (Rolex or Ferrari), or how a name became the standard for everything else (Kleenex or Post-It Note). Many companies spend a great deal of time building their brands, and some brands are, in and of themselves, valued in the billions of dollars.

When someone takes that brand and uses it illegally, it tarnishes the brand's image and can decrease its value. It can also lead to higher prices for consumers due to legal action, tighter security for Web sites, or legitimate communications with customers to inform them of an ongoing scam.

Basically, phishing scams cost everyone money, not just their victims.

Protect yourself

The following are a few ways to protect yourself from phishing scams based upon recommendations from The Anti-Phishing Working Group (APWG), a group of individuals and companies that fight against online fraud.

- **The simple things**—If you've never bought anything from a company (Ebay, for example) chances are you won't be getting an e-mail from them. But if you have done business with the company and aren't sure of the e-mail, look for incorrect spellings and poor-quality images often found in phishing schemes.

- **No rush**—It is highly unlikely that any legitimate company will tell you, without prior warning, to contact them immediately; most will give you a few days. So beware of e-mail messages that request immediate action, since that could be an indication of a scam.

- **Protect your information**—No company will ever ask for your Social Security number, account number, or password via e-mail or even over the phone; they will only do so from secure sites when online, and will only ask for a simple identifier over the phone (e.g. the last four digits of your Social Security number, not the whole thing).

- **Ignore the links**—If you're not sure about an e-mail, never click on a link it contains. It is possible to make one Web site address look like a different one. (For example, it may look like you are on www.your-bank.com, but in reality you are on www.phisher-site.com.) Instead, either use a bookmark or type in the real site address.

You can find more information on this issue at www.antiphishing.org. And, one last piece of advice:

- **When all else fails**—If you're not sure what to do, just call the company in question. Odds are they'll help if it is a real problem, and you can notify them of the phishing scam if not.

Your help is needed

The easy thing to do is just delete any phishing e-mail you receive. Doing so, however, won't make the problem go away, since no one else will know what you received, where it actually came from, or who is responsible. For this reason, it's absolutely imperative that consumers report the phishing e-mails they receive, and it's quite easy to do:

- **Mark it as spam**—Most of the large providers (Yahoo!, Hotmail, etc.) have a button you can simply click to notify them the e-mail you received is spam. From there, the sender's information is entered into a database that can help the e-mail provider stop similar scams in the future.
- **Notify your e-mail provider**—If you have been absolutely overloaded by phishing e-mails, contact your e-mail provider directly and report the abusive messages.
- **Contact APWG**—You can also send the message on to the Anti-Phishing Working Group using the guidelines on their Web site: www.antiphishing.org/report_phishing.html

By reporting these messages, you help build a database of offenders, provide valuable information that can stop new types of attacks, and save companies and consumers millions of dollars.

Remember, phishing scams affect everyone—military and civilian, rich and poor, young and old, company and customer. But by taking a few steps to protect yourself and reporting the messages you receive, you can make a difference and help put phishers out of business.

Resources

The following Web sites contain facts and figures used in this book, and can offer you more detailed information on a wide range of financial issues.

- **www.pioneerservices.com**—Information about Pioneer Services, as well as free financial education articles, debt payment calculators, and other information.
- **www.carfax.com**—If you're buying a used car, you can run your own vehicle history report.
- **www.autoweb.com**—Find prices on thousands of new and used cars.
- **www.carbuyingtips.com**—A wealth of information on tips to save money, scams to avoid, and links to helpful sites.
- **www.car.com**—Get an up-front, no obligation price quote from a dealer near you, as well as helpful and informative articles.
- **www.military.com/Finance/CarBuying**—Helpful tips on saving money, facts on leasing vs. buying, and other useful information.
- **www.edmunds.com**—Find out how much a car is really worth with this consumer-friendly site.
- **www.students.gov**—A portal into federal dollars for education, information about employment, and other issues concerning students.
- **www.pueblo.gsa.gov**—Helpful information about 529 plans.
- **www.collegboard.com**—General information about college costs.
- **www.salliemae.com**—The largest provider of student loans in the country.
- **www.annualcreditreport.com**—The only site officially designated to give you one free copy of your report from each bureau every year.

- www.equifax.com—One of the three main credit bureaus.
- www.experian.com—One of the three main credit bureaus.
- www.transunion.com—One of the three main credit bureaus.
- www.identitytheft911.com and www.idtheftcenter.org—Both of these sites offer resources and information and how to recover from and combat identity theft.
- www.creditcards.com/Holiday-Spending-Can-Lead-to-Financial-Hangovers.php—Used in Chapter 11.
- www.msnbc.msn.com/id/15835045/—News story about consumer debt during the 2006 holiday season.
- www.cnn.com/2007/US/01/03/debt.holiday.hangover.ap/index.html—Another story about holiday debt, this time from CNN.
- www.responsiblelending.org/pdfs/rr012exec-Financial_Quicksand-1106.pdf—A report by the Center for Responsible Lending on the dangers of payday loans.

Glossary

The following are some basic terms and definitions that can give you a better understanding of your finances.

Algorithm: A mathematical model used in credit scoring to compare data in a person's report and predict his or her likelihood of repaying his or her debts. The higher the credit score, the better.

Annual Percentage Rate (APR): A calculation that defines the total cost of a loan or line of credit, including all interest and fees. This will often be higher than the interest rate since it includes the fees.

Bankruptcy: A legal proceeding designed to help people in severe financial difficulty get a fresh start by relieving them of some of their current debts. Bankruptcies usually stay on a credit report for 7 to 10 years.

Charge-off: An unpaid portion of a bill that a lender has accepted will never be paid and has been recorded on the books as a bad debt. It is a serious negative item on a credit report.

Collection: A creditor's attempt to recover a past-due payment by turning the account over to a collection department or company. Having a debt in collection is a serious negative item on a credit report.

Credit bureau: A credit-reporting agency that is a clearinghouse for information on the credit rating of individuals or companies. It is often called a "credit repository" or "consumer reporting agency." The three largest are Equifax, Experian and TransUnion.

Equifax
1-800-685-1111
Credit Information Services
PO Box 740241
Atlanta, GA 30374
www.equifax.com

Experian
1-888-397-3742
National Consumer Assistance Center
PO Box 2104
Allen, TX 75013
www.experian.com

Trans Union
1-800-888-4213
Consumer Disclosure Center
PO Box 1000
Chester, PA 19022
www.transunion.com

Credit history: A record of a person's use of credit over time.

Credit limit: The most that can be charged on a credit card or a credit line.

Credit report: A document containing financial information about a person, focusing on his or her history of paying obligations. It includes current balances on outstanding debts, the individual's amount of available credit, public records such as bankruptcies, and inquiries about credit from various companies.

Credit risk: The measure of a person's creditworthiness. People who are more likely to repay their debts on time are considered less of a risk by lenders, and will be charged lower interest rates for borrowing money. Those with a history of failing to pay debt on time are considered a higher risk and are charged more for borrowing money.

Debt-to-income ratio: The amount of money a person has in outstanding debt, compared to the amount of income a person has. The higher a person's debt ratio, the more risky the individual appears to potential lenders. Anything below 40 percent is considered positive by most lenders.

Debt Cycle: A condition or situation borrowers can find themselves in when they continue to borrow more money than they are able to repay, thus increasing their debt. "Breaking the debt cycle" is a common reference in describing financial strategies to pay off seemingly endless debt.

Default: A designation on a credit report that indicates a person has not paid a debt. Accounts usually are listed as being in default after several reports of delinquency. Defaults are very serious and are considered as negatives on a credit report.

Delinquent: A designation on a credit report that means a person hasn't made the minimum payment on a debt on time. On credit reports, delinquencies are usually shown as being 30, 60, 90 or 120 days delinquent. Delinquencies are a seriously negative item on a credit report.

FICO score: The most commonly used credit score. The name comes from the Fair Isaac Corporation, which developed the scoring model, and is used to predict the likelihood that a person will pay his or her debts.

Grace Period: Typically describes the time you have before a credit card company starts charging you interest on your new purchases. Not every card offers one, some cards do but have restrictions, and the length of the grace period varies. This information will be listed in the disclosure when you first received your card.

Hard inquiry: An item on a person's credit report that indicates that someone has asked for a copy of the individual's report. Hard inquiries are requests that result from a person applying for credit, and are included in the formula for determining a person's credit score.

Installment credit: A type of credit in which the monthly payment is the same every month and the time period to repay the loan is fixed, such as a basic loan.

Interest rate: The fee charged by a lender for the use of the borrowed money, usually expressed as a percentage of the total amount borrowed. The interest rate is dependent upon many factors, including rates charged by the Federal Reserve Board and the past credit history of the borrower.

Judgment: A decision from a judge on a civil action or lawsuit that is usually an amount of money a person is required to pay to satisfy a debt or a penalty.

Lien: A legal claim placed on a person's property, such as a car or a house, as security for a debt. Example: A contractor may place a lien on a house after they did work and didn't get paid, and the property cannot be sold without the lien being paid first.

Public record: Information on your credit report that has been obtained from court records, such as bankruptcies, judgments, and liens.

Rate shopping: Applying for credit with several lenders to find the best interest rate, usually for a mortgage or a car loan. This will show up on a credit report but, if done within a short period of time (such as two weeks), it should have little impact on a credit score.

Revolving credit: A type of credit line that does not have a fixed number of payments or payoff date, such as a credit card.

Soft inquiry: An item on a person's credit report that indicates that someone has asked for a copy of his or her report. Soft inquiries can be from current creditors reviewing the file, prospective creditors who want to send out an offer (such as a pre-approved credit card), or a person's own review of their file. They are not included in the formula for determining a person's credit score.

Trade line: An account listed on a credit report. Each separate account is a different trade line.

Unsecured Loan: A loan that is not backed by collateral; sometimes called a "signature" or "note" loan.

978-0-595-47777-7
0-595-47777-1

Printed in the United States
108402LV00002B/1-249/P